Flannel Quilts

Flannel Quilts

Sandy Bonsib

Martingale™
& COMPANY

Credits

President . . . . Nancy J. Martin
CEO . . . . Daniel J. Martin
Publisher . . . . Jane Hamada
Editorial Director . . . . Mary V. Green
Editorial Project Manager . . . . Tina Cook
Technical Editor . . . . Ursula Reikes
Copy Editor . . . . Pamela Mostek
Design and Production Manager . . . . Stan Green
Illustrator . . . . Robin Strobel
Cover and Text Designer . . . . Regina Girard
Photographer . . . . Brent Kane

That Patchwork Place® is an imprint of Martingale & Company™.

Flannel Quilts
© 2001 by Sandy Bonsib

Martingale & Company
20205 144th Ave. NE
Woodinville, WA 98072-8478 USA
www.martingale-pub.com

Printed in Singapore
06 05 04 03 02 01   8 7 6 5 4 3 2 1

Mission Statement

We are dedicated to providing quality products and service by working together to inspire creativity and to enrich the lives we touch.

Library of Congress Cataloging-in-Publication Data
Bonsib, Sandy.
    Flannel quilts / Sandy Bonsib
        p. cm.
    ISBN 1-56477-360-4
        1. Patchwork–Patterns. 2. Patchwork quilts.
3. Quilting. 4. Flannel. I. Title

TT835 .B6277 2001
746.46'041–dc21

                                    2001031524

Dedication

This book is dedicated to everyone who works at In The Beginning Fabrics in Seattle, Washington. Over the past ten years, you have been my co-workers, friends, and supporters. With you, I have both laughed and cried. Over the years, you have supported me in so many ways. As I have made quilts for my books and for my classes, you have helped me choose fabrics and brainstorm ideas, and offered wonderful suggestions throughout the process.

You all have helped our monthly volunteer group for more than two years as we have worked to make over four hundred quilts in just twenty-four months for the children of battered women.

You have welcomed my guide-dog puppies into your hearts, been a part of their training, grown to love them, and been sad, along with me, when it was time to say good-bye so they could return to Guide Dogs for the Blind for advanced training.

Thank you so much to each and every one of you, and especially to longtime colleagues Trish Carey, Margy Duncan, Betty Eckstein, Kelly Hogan, Vicki Hurst, Kristine Kerschner, Kathie Koepsell, Leah Nelson, Jackie Quinn, Diane Roubal, Laurie Shifrin, Mary Jo Sisley, and Gale Whitney. And a special thank you to Sharon and Jason Yenter, owners of In The Beginning. You all make what I do so much easier and so much more fun.

Acknowledgments

Without the help of my husband, John Bickley, and my teenagers, Ben and Kate, I would never be able to write books. They help me with endless details as I work, and they take over many daily chores so I can meet my deadlines. Even after more than twenty years, John is still the nicest person I know. Ben, my resident computer genius, has known how to fix any computer problem I've ever had. Kate must have baked a million chocolate chip cookies to keep my students happy in the last few months. She is also my consultant about fabrics, settings, and border choices. Her ideas make my work so much easier, so much more fun, and my quilts so much better.

Thank you to my friends Kathy Staley and Lynn Ahlers, who helped me so much in so many ways as I made the quilts for this book. Lynn helped bind quilts, and Kathy helped cut fabrics, pick up and deliver quilts to Becky Kraus (my machine quilter) and bind so many quilts that I've lost count. Many thanks to the rest of my quilt group, the Flannel Folks and Button Babes, for being ready to help me if I needed it.

Thank you to Becky Kraus. She has machine quilted so many quilts for me over the years, and I continue to appreciate her creative ideas and beautiful workmanship. I don't know how I'd make quilts without her.

Thank you to Margy Duncan for permission to use her pattern "Gingersnap Nine Patch" for one of my flannel quilts. It is one of my favorites.

Thank you to Beverly Dunivent, quilt teacher, historian, and AQS certified appraiser, for sharing with me both information about the history of flannel and for loaning me the flannel flag and American Indian motif, both of which are almost one hundred years old.

Thank you to Trish Carey, my mentor and dear friend. Mentors are hard to come by, and she's the best.

Thank you to my many students around the country who have taken my classes and made wonderful quilts. I have learned as much from you as you have from me.

A special thank you to Ursula Reikes, my editor for all four of my books, for her patience, understanding, and expert skills—and for being a good friend, as well.

Finally, thank you to Martingale & Company for once again believing in me.

Contents

Introduction ~ 8

Flannel Fabrics ~ 9
What Is Flannel? ~ 9
Selecting Flannels ~ 9
Prewashing Flannels ~ 11

Basic Guidelines ~ 12
Supplies ~ 12
Parts of a Quilt ~ 13
Rotary Cutting ~ 14
Cutting Triangles ~ 15
Piecing ~ 16
Piecing Half-Square-Triangle Units ~ 16
Pinning ~ 17
Pressing ~ 17
Appliqué ~ 18
Squaring Up the Blocks ~ 20
Assembling the Quilt Top ~ 20
Making Quilts Larger ~ 22

Tips and Tricks for Working
with Flannels ~ 23

The Patterns ~ 25
100 Squares ~ 26
Blue-Work Babies ~ 28
Family Flannels ~ 31
Easy Four Patch Hearts ~ 34
Hearts in the Garden ~ 37

Almost Amish ~ 41
Playful Puppies ~ 44
Wear Your Shades, Baby! This Quilt Is
Bright! ~ 48
Hot Chocolate and a Storybook ~ 51
Baby Animals for Baby ~ 56
Dynamic Duo:
Plaid and Floral Stars ~ 59
Folk Flowers ~ 62
Color! Color! Color! ~ 66
Plaid Nine Patch ~ 69
Old-Fashioned Baskets ~ 72
Circle Around ~ 75
Flannel Sampler ~ 78

Finishing the Quilt ~ 87
Adding Borders ~ 87
Backing ~ 89
Batting ~ 89
Making the Quilt Sandwich ~ 90
Quilting ~ 90
Binding ~ 92
Adding a Label ~ 93
Embellishing with Buttons ~ 93

Bibliography ~ 94

About the Author ~ 95

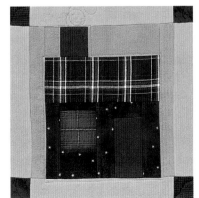

Introduction

Historically, flannel fabrics have been around since the late 1800s. Between about 1875 and 1925, plaid and striped cotton flannels were used as a distinctive quilt-backing fabric and can be found on the back of many wool quilts and foundation quilts from that era. In the early 1900s, flannels intended to be used on the front of a quilt included motifs such as those shown below.

Today, there are more flannels available than ever before. Quilters can choose many different colors and styles, including '30s prints, florals, novelty prints for both children and adults, bright and pale pastels and solids, as well as traditional baby flannels, plaids, and stripes. Some flannels are even "two-sided"—flannel on one side and homespun on the other—giving you a choice of which side to use.

In this book, you'll find complete directions for making seventeen quilts. The flannels used in these quilts are diverse, colorful, and eye-catching. A smaller sample block accompanies some of the quilts, showing another color option for that quilt. Most quilts feature simple traditional blocks, perhaps with a slight variation from the original, and vary in number of blocks from four to twenty per quilt. Because the blocks are large, the quilts go together quickly; most can be finished in a single day. For teachers and those who love sampler quilts, there is a quilt using many of the 10" blocks featured in this book.

In addition to the basics, this book presents many new ways to use this wonderful fabric. To mention a few, you can combine flannels with regular cotton fabrics, show off plaids in a block by cutting them on the bias, and use flannel as a batting to create a lightweight summer quilt.

Comprehensive information about working with flannels includes guidelines for washing, handling, sewing, and pressing. Although the flannels used in this book are 100 percent cotton, they are different from regular cotton. Flannel has nap, it stretches, it shrinks more than regular cotton, and it creates extra bulk in seam allowances. Yet, contrary to what you may think, flannel is an easy fabric to work with. The tips and tricks on page 23 should solve any problems you might have had in the past. After learning the basics, flannel will become one of your favorite fabrics.

According to noted quilt historian Merikay Waldvogel, "these flannels were probably designed for chewing tobacco or loose tobacco containers. The most familiar tobacco flannels were the international flags...but other flannels featured baseball players, college teams, Indian blankets, Kewpie dolls and nursery rhyme figures."

The exact date of these samples is not certain but we know that most flags that had 48 stars came into use in 1912. Again, according to Waldvogel, "By 1917, all four major tobacco companies had stopped including pictorial silk ribbons, flannels, and cards inside the packages." Thus we can assume that these flannel pieces are at least 84 years old.

Flannel Fabrics

What Is Flannel?

Flannel is a soft, woven cloth of wool, cotton, a blend of wool and cotton, or synthetics. *Flannelette* more specifically defines what we usually call flannel today. *Flannelette* is a soft cotton cloth with a nap. When looking for definitions of flannel, I also came across the term "outing flannel," defined as a soft, lightweight cotton fabric, usually with a short nap on both sides (not just one side like the flannels we usually use in our quilts).

Flannel is created by a mechanical finishing process called napping. This process is applied to one or both sides of a fabric. It raises the fiber ends to the surface. Originally used to create a softer finish on wool, napping today is also applied to cotton and man-made fibers.

In general, napped fabrics are warmer and more stain-resistant than fabrics with no nap. They often reflect light differently when held in different positions. They can vary in weight and in the amount of nap, from cotton flannel, which has a soft, light fuzz, to wool coating fabrics with very thick naps. In addition to cotton flannel, other napped fabrics include wool broadcloth, wool flannel, doeskin, serge, camel hair, mohair, cotton outing, sweatshirt fleece, suede cloth, brushed denim, and lamb's wool.

For more information on how flannel fabrics are produced, see Harriet Hargrave's book, *From Fiber to Fabric* (see "Bibliography" on page 94).

Selecting Flannels

The guidelines for selecting flannels are similar to those for selecting any fabrics for a quilt. I tend to buy flannels that I like when I see them, because they might not still be there by the time I'm actually ready to use them. Like all fabrics, flannels go in and out of style, with many fabrics being made for only one season.

You may have noticed that flannels often vary in weight, from the very lightweight, to reversible flannel/homespun fabrics, to the thicker, heavier flannels. I don't hesitate to mix different weights as long as I've preshrunk everything. Extra thickness of a particular fabric will sink into the batting once the quilt is quilted, and you'll never know that their weights varied. However, if you prefer to work with similar weights, then do so. It may limit your choices, but as with most things in quilting, there's not a right or a wrong way. Use your judgment and do what you feel comfortable doing.

When making flannel quilts, consider adding 100 percent–cotton, nonflannel fabrics if you can't find a flannel in a color or pattern that you need. In "Color! Color! Color!" (page 66), I found that I couldn't get a full range of color with just flannel fabrics, so I substituted a few cotton nonflannels throughout the quilt. In "Old-fashioned Baskets" (page 72), I used a nonflannel rose print for the alternate blocks and the side and corner triangles. I couldn't find a flannel fabric that I liked better with the neutral baskets. As long as both the flannels and nonflannels are 100 percent–cotton and both have been preshrunk, they can be combined in the same quilt. Don't feel limited to flannel fabrics only. If a nonflannel fabric makes your flannel quilt sing, use it.

Because so many flannel quilts are meant to be used, and are often used until they are worn-out, buy good-quality flannels. How can you tell? Feel them. I avoid flannels that feel like cardboard. Flannels that are soft are of higher quality. You can also look on the end of the bolt. Flannels made by reputable companies should wear very well.

When selecting fabrics for any quilt, consider the following:

- **Vary the values** (the lightness or darkness of a fabric). You won't be able to see the design of your block when it's hanging on a wall or covering a bed if the fabrics that you sew together don't have enough contrast.

Poor contrast   *Good contrast*   *Good contrast*

- **Vary the scale** of the prints and plaids. Large-scale prints and plaids often look good in larger areas, such as borders. However, when combined with small- and medium-scale prints in the same block, large-scale prints help to show off the smaller prints.

Combine varying scales of prints and plaids.

- Don't be afraid to **mix prints, plaids, and stripes** in one quilt. It is the mix of different designs that adds interest. Plaids and stripes provide wonderful contrast to nongeometric prints, and vice versa.

Create visual texture with multiple print patterns.

- **Look for motifs**—in novelty prints and other large-scale prints that you can feature in the center of a block.

Take advantage of pattern motifs in your blocks.

Fussy Cutting

To isolate and "fussy cut" a motif, use a window template to determine what size will work best with your fabric. Sometimes the size that looks good will surprise you. Using three pieces of paper, cut a square out of the center of each one: make one 2" x 2", one 3" x 3", and one 4" x 4" window. To use the window templates, move each template around the fabric to isolate a motif. Choose the one that looks best and draw lightly on the fabric with a pencil, inside the square; then remove the template. Add a ¼"-wide seam allowance all around and cut out the square. You can also just mark the corners, being sure to add a ¼" seam allowance all around. Fussy cutting is easiest to do with a square ruler. It's always wise, and often a time-saver, to check the size before you cut.

Cutting specific designs from fabric requires extra yardage. Plan your cuts carefully.

Prewashing Flannels

It is important to prewash flannels before using them. Because the weave is more open, flannels often shrink at twice the rate, or more, of regular cottons. Generally, regular cottons shrink 1" per yard, whereas flannels can shrink 2" to 3" per yard. Some flannels continue to shrink after the first wash. So, to achieve maximum shrinkage, I recommend washing and drying flannel fabric twice; wash it, dry it, then wash and dry again. Most of the shrinkage will occur with the first wash, and less with the second wash.

Flannels do fray, and two washings and two dryings can cause considerable fraying. There are a number of ways to handle this problem. One is to prewash your flannels in the sink, wringing out excess water with your hands; then dry the flannels in the dryer. With this method, you avoid the agitation of the washer, which contributes to the fraying. Another way to control the fraying is to place your fabrics in a hosiery bag or a pillow cover with a zipper when you wash them in the washing machine. This will protect the fabrics during agitation in the washer. Remove the fabrics from the protective bag before putting them in the dryer, except for small pieces, which you can leave in the bag while drying.

The second shrinkage is comparable to the shrinkage in nonflannel fabrics, so if you like the slightly puffy look of your grandmother's quilts, wash your flannels only once. Then they will shrink just a little when you wash the finished quilt for the first time.

Once your flannels are washed and dried, iron them. Flannels usually need to be ironed to make them wrinkle-free enough for cutting.

Basic Guidelines

Supplies

You will need the following basic supplies to make the quilts in this book:

- 100 percent–cotton flannels
- 100 percent–cotton nonflannels as desired
- 100 percent–cotton sewing thread
- 100 percent–cotton batting in your choice of thickness
- Cotton thread and/or pearl cotton for machine or hand quilting
- Buttons for some quilts
- Sewing machine in good working order, with a walking foot if you plan to machine quilt
- Straight pins
- Seam ripper
- Marking pencil
- Safety pins if you plan to machine quilt
- Rotary cutting equipment, including:
  - Medium-sized or large-sized rotary cutter
  - Cutting mat, 17" x 23" (minimum size)
  - 6" x 24" Omnigrid ruler
- A variety of rulers in different sizes can be helpful. A 12½" x 12½" square ruler is great for cutting larger pieces or for squaring up blocks. A 6" x 12" ruler works well for smaller pieces, and an 8" bias square is handy for trimming half-square triangles.

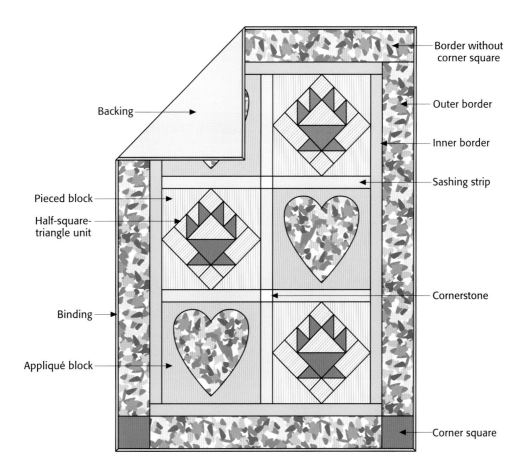

Backing

Border without corner square

Outer border

Inner border

Sashing strip

Pieced block

Half-square-triangle unit

Cornerstone

Binding

Appliqué block

Corner square

Parts of a Quilt

Pieced Blocks: Pieces of fabric in various sizes and shapes sewn together to form a larger design.

Half-Square-Triangle Unit: A square made up of two triangles.

Appliqué Block: Fabric shapes stitched on top of a pieced or unpieced background.

Sashing: Strips of fabric sewn between the blocks and between rows of blocks.

Cornerstone: Square of fabric sewn between sashing strips.

Border: The area surrounding the main body of the quilt top, acting much like the frame of a picture. One or more fabric strips of varying widths may be added. The first border is generally called the inner border. Depending on how many borders are added, the second border might be the middle border or the outer border.

Corner Square: A square of fabric or a pieced block that joins adjacent border strips.

Batting (not shown): The puffy layer inside the quilt, sandwiched between the quilt top and the quilt backing and held in place by stitches made by hand or by machine.

Backing: A large piece of fabric, possibly seamed from smaller pieces, that covers the back of a quilt.

Binding: A strip of fabric, cut either on the straight grain or the bias grain, sewn to and wrapped around the edges of the quilt.

Rotary Cutting

Directions are for rotary cutting all pieces, and all measurements include a ¼"-wide seam allowance. The blade on a rotary cutter is very sharp. Keep it away from children and remember to use the safety guard after every cut.

1. Fold the fabric, wrong sides together, aligning the crosswise and lengthwise grains as much as possible. Smooth your fabric to flatten it. The selvages will not line up. Sometimes they will be very skewed. Don't worry about that. Place the folded edge closest to you on the cutting mat.

Note: Most quilters expect the selvages of folded fabric to line up, but after you prewash flannels, the selvages usually do not line up. Why? Remember that the cloth used to make flannel is woven with yarns that have fairly loose fibers. Although the warp yarns are strong, the filling yarns are loose, to make napping easy. What this means to a quilter is that when flannel shrinks, the warp yarns shrink less than the filling yarns, often creating a funny, definitely "unsquare" shape. Trying to square up your fabric by aligning the selvages doesn't work. If you force the selvages to line up, your fabric won't lie flat, which makes it difficult to cut a straight strip. The best thing to do is to fold and smooth the fabric without worrying about the selvages. This is what I do. Does this mean that sometimes the fabric is cut a little off-grain? Sometimes, yes, but keep in mind that when you are making a quilt, most long strips become smaller pieces in a block. And each piece, after it is sewn to other pieces in the block, will be stabilized on all sides with a seam. This will hold a slightly off-grain piece of fabric in place. Also, when the quilting is done, more stitching is added through all three layers, further stabilizing a piece that's not perfectly on-grain.

2. Align a square ruler along the folded edge of the fabric. Place a 24" ruler to the left of the square, just covering the uneven raw edges of the fabric. Remove the square ruler and cut along the right-hand edge of the ruler, rolling the rotary cutter away from you. Discard this first strip, which is called the "cleanup cut." Reverse this procedure if you are left-handed.

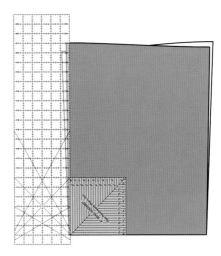

3. To cut strips, align the required measurement on the ruler with the newly cut edge of the fabric. For example, to cut a 2½"-wide strip, place the 2½" mark of the ruler on the edge of the fabric.

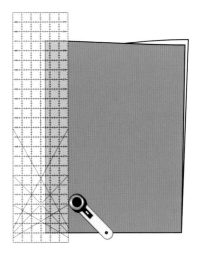

4. To cut squares and rectangles, cut strips in the required widths. Remove the selvage ends of the strip. Align the required measurements on the ruler with the left edge of the strip and cut a square or rectangle. Continue cutting until you have the required number of pieces.

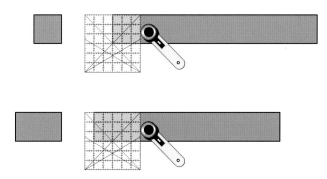

5. For some quilts, you will cut strips, sew them together in strip sets, and then cut segments from the strip sets. First, trim the ends of the strip set to square it up (this is your cleanup cut). Then, align the required measurement on the ruler with the left edge of the strip set and cut the specified number of segments.

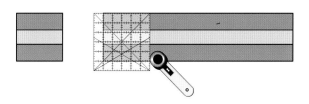

Cutting Triangles

Two different types of triangles are used in this book. The difference between them is the direction of the straight grain. On half-square triangles, the straight grain is on the short sides. On quarter-square triangles, it is on the long side.

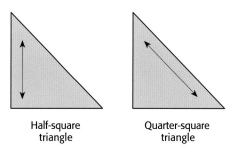

Half-square triangle   Quarter-square triangle

For half-square triangles, cut a square the size indicated in the cutting chart. Cut the square once diagonally. This symbol ◻ is used to indicate when to cut half-square triangles.

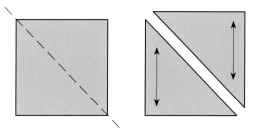

For quarter-square triangles, cut a square the size indicated in the cutting chart. Cut the square twice diagonally as follows: cut it once and don't move either piece; then line up the ruler on the opposite diagonal and cut again. This symbol ⊠ is used to indicate when to cut quarter-square triangles.

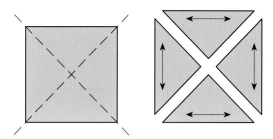

Piecing

The single most important thing to do when making quilts is to maintain a consistent ¼"-wide seam allowance throughout your piecing. Otherwise, your block will not be the desired finished size. If that happens, the size of everything else in the quilt is affected—alternate blocks, sashing, and borders. Measurements for all components of the quilt are based on blocks that finish to the desired size plus ¼" all around for seams.

Creating an Accurate Seam Guide

Take the time to establish an exact ¼"-wide seam guide on your machine. Some sewing machines have a special ¼" foot, which means you can use the edge of the presser foot to guide the edge of the fabric for a perfect ¼"-wide seam.

If you don't have such a foot, don't despair. You can easily create a seam guide with masking tape or electrical tape. Electrical tape is available in different colors that contrast with the color of your machine, making the tape easy to see.

Place a ruler under your presser foot. Gently lower the needle onto the first ¼" line from the right-hand edge of the ruler. Place a piece of tape along the right-hand edge of the ruler, in front of the needle, as shown.

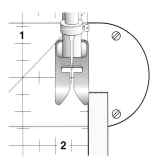

Test your new guide to make sure your seams are ¼" wide; if they are not, readjust your seam guide. Many quilters find that they need to take a scant ¼" seam rather than a full measured ¼" to get their blocks the right size.

Piecing Half-Square-Triangle Units

I use two methods to make half-square-triangle units. Both of them avoid sewing the triangles on their bias edges.

Sew and Flip

Cut squares the size given in the quilt directions. Pair two squares with right sides together, and draw a diagonal line on the wrong side of the lighter square. Stitch on the diagonal line. Press one triangle over so the right side is visible. On the side that now has three layers of fabric, trim the seam allowance to ¼" on the bottom two layers, removing the triangles under the stitched unit. Each pair of squares yields one half-square-triangle unit.

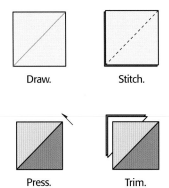

Draw.   Stitch.

Press.   Trim.

I also use the sew-and-flip method to create star points (see "Dynamic Duo" on page 59). Following a similar procedure, draw a diagonal line on the wrong side of the square. Position the square as indicated in the project directions and sew on the diagonal line. Trim the seam allowance to ¼" and remove the back two layers of fabric. Press the triangle toward the corner of the square or rectangle.

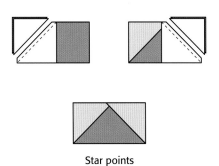

Star points

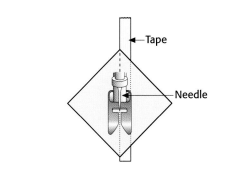
Two for One

Cut squares the size given in the quilt directions. Pair two squares with right sides together; draw a diagonal line on the wrong side of the lighter square. This is not your sewing line; it will become your cutting line. Draw another set of lines ¼" from the drawn line. These are your sewing lines. (It is not necessary to draw the sewing lines if you have a ¼" presser foot.) Stitch ¼" away from the center line on both sides. Cut on the center line. Press seam allowances toward the darker fabric. Each pair of squares yields two half-square-triangle units. I often make these units slightly larger than required; then I trim them to the needed size.

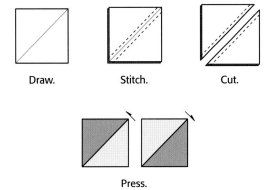

Draw. Stitch. Cut.

Press.

Pinning

Take the time to pin pieces together when assembling blocks. There is a tendency for the pieces to shift slightly as they are fed under the presser foot, and this is especially true for flannels because of the nap. A few carefully placed pins will keep the shifting to a minimum. I sew right over the pins, removing them after I've stitched a seam. Although I was cautioned many years ago that I'd break needles that way, that happens very seldom to me. If you prefer, you can remove pins as you come to them.

Pressing

I use an iron on a cotton setting and steam to press the seams and the blocks. While steam can cause some distortion, it creates flat seams and blocks. Of course, flannel, with its open weave, will distort even more than regular cottons. So, if you prefer, do not use steam with flannel, and see if you like the results. Press each seam after stitching and before adding other pieces.

Press seams to one side, usually toward the darker of the two fabrics. Pressing arrows are provided in illustrations where the direction in which you press your seams is important. Following these arrows will make constructing the blocks and assembling the quilt top easier. However, with flannels, you may want to try ironing the seam open to reduce bulk. Try both methods and do what feels right for you.

Appliqué

Flannel is surprisingly easy to appliqué. Its additional thickness creates a crisp edge, even on curves. And appliqué stitches become truly invisible because they are hidden in the nap.

There are two methods I like to use when appliquéing flannel. The first is needle-turn appliqué. This method takes more time and requires a little practice, but I find it quite easy to do with flannel. The second method, I call it pocket appliqué, works best on very simple shapes. It is easy to do, faster than needle-turn, and provides a finished edge on large appliqué shapes.

Needle-Turn Appliqué

1. Make a plastic template of the appliqué shape. With a pencil, trace around the template (placed right side up) on the right side of the appliqué fabric.

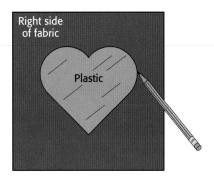

2. Cut out the shape, adding a scant ¼" seam allowance all around the outline as you cut.

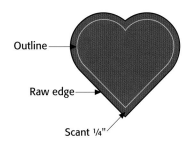

3. Position the shape on the background fabric and pin in place.

4. Starting on a straight edge, use the tip of the needle to turn under the ¼" seam allowance, about ½" at a time. Turn under just enough of the scant ¼" seam allowance so that the pencil line on the appliqué piece doesn't show.

5. Holding the turned seam allowance firmly between your thumb and index finger, stitch the appliqué to the background. I use a back whipstitch with needle-turn appliqué. The stitch is similar to a hem stitch, except the needle is inserted into the background fabric just a couple of threads behind where the thread came out of the shape.

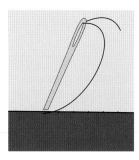

Pocket Appliqué

This is a quick way to turn under the seam allowances on large, simple shapes. I used it to make the flowers in "Folk Flowers" (page 62).

1. Fold a piece of fabric with rights sides facing. Trace the template on the wrong side of the folded fabric.

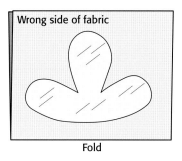

2. Keeping the layers together, stitch on the drawn line. Cut around the shape, leaving a ¼" seam allowance. Just eyeball it; you don't need to measure it. Clip the cleavages and trim the fabric around the point, if there is one, to a little less than ¼".

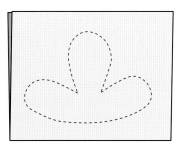

3. Make a small slit on one side. Turn the shape inside out and press. The reason I use two layers of the same fabric is so that I don't have to be a perfect presser. If a little bit of the back fabric shows beyond the edge of the shape, you'll never notice it because the fabric is the same on both sides. To eliminate the extra bulk of having two layers, you can cut out the back layer, leaving a ¼" seam allowance. However, I usually leave my appliqués doubled because I like the dimensional look when the appliqué "pops out" more than usual from the background.

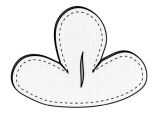

4. Stitch the shape to the background with a back whipstitch and regular thread, or with No. 8 pearl cotton and a running stitch, blanket stitch, or other stitch of your choice.

Running stitch appliqué

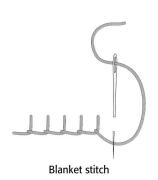

Blanket stitch appliqué

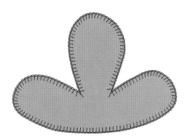

Blanket stitch

Squaring Up the Blocks

No matter how carefully you sew, some blocks may end up a little smaller or a little larger than the required size. This is especially true of flannel blocks since the fabric stretches more than most cottons. Trying to sew different-sized blocks together is very frustrating. You can do a certain amount of easing, depending on the size of the block. But trimming the blocks to the same size will make sewing them together so much easier.

To square up your blocks, measure each block. Determine which block is the smallest and trim the other blocks to match. Although you may not reduce the block size significantly, the change will affect the sashing strips and borders. For example, most blocks in this book are 10½" (including seam allowances). If some of yours are as small as 10¼" or as large as 10¾", you will be able to ease them together, and you won't need to square up the blocks. But if some blocks are as small as 10", you will want to cut all the blocks down to 10". If there are sashing strips, you will also have to cut these down to fit the 10" block. Similar adjustments will need to be made for borders. When in doubt, measure your quilt through the center before cutting border strips.

Use a rotary cutter and a square ruler to trim the blocks. The important thing to remember is that you need to remove equal amounts from all sides. For example, if you need to trim a 10½" block down to 10", you need to remove ¼" from all four sides, or if you're starting with a 10¼" block, you need to remove ⅛" from all four sides.

Caution: If triangle points come to the edge of your finished block, be careful about trimming the seam allowance. Trimming these blocks may mean the points of your triangles will be cut off when the block is sewn to another piece of fabric.

Assembling the Quilt Top

When you have made all the blocks and cut all the remaining pieces, it's time to put them together to make the quilt top.

Arrange the blocks, following the illustration or directions provided with each quilt. It is helpful to use a design wall, which is an extra-thick piece of fleece you can attach to a wall temporarily. Not only will your quilt blocks stick to the design wall without pinning, but the biggest advantage of a design wall is that it is a vertical surface, so all your blocks are the same distance from your eye. When you arrange your blocks on the floor, some blocks are closer to you, some are farther away. A vertical surface gives you a better perspective, and you can more readily decide if your blocks look balanced. Do you have too many lights, brights, or dark fabrics in the same place? Is a particularly eye-catching color or pattern distributed evenly throughout the quilt?

For straight-set quilts, join the blocks in horizontal rows. Press seams in opposite directions from row to row so opposing seams will butt up against each other when you join the rows. Pressing arrows are provided to show you the ideal pressing direction for the seams. Join the rows, making sure to match the seams between the blocks. Secure with a pin if desired.

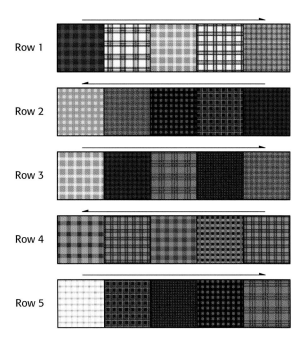

Row 1

Row 2

Row 3

Row 4

Row 5

For quilts with sashing strips, refer to the color photo and the diagrams to arrange the blocks and sashing strips. Join the blocks and vertical sashing strips in rows; press seams toward the sashing strips. Then join the rows and horizontal sashing strips.

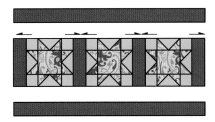

For diagonally set quilts, refer to the project photo and diagrams to arrange the blocks and sashing strips (if applicable) in diagonal rows. Sew the blocks into rows, adding a side triangle at each end. Join the diagonal rows and add the corner triangles last.

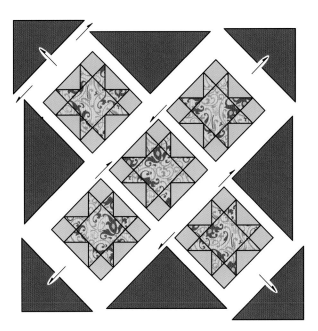

For diagonally set quilts, I cut the side and corner triangles larger than necessary; then I trim the edges to straighten them. I do this for two reasons. First, oversized triangles create "float," which is an area between the block points and the first border. It creates the illusion that the blocks are floating on the background. Second, when the blocks float I don't have to worry about the corners of the blocks getting cut off when I add the borders.

To create the float and straighten the edges, you will need to trim all four sides of the quilt top after it is completed. To do this, place a long ruler on the block points at the measurement specified in the directions. For example, in the diagram below, the 1½" mark on the ruler is placed on the block points and the excess is trimmed with a rotary cutter. This means that after the first border is added, there will be a float of 1¼" between the corners of the blocks and the first border.

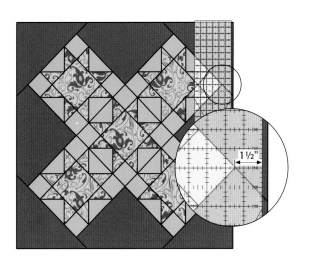

Making Quilts Larger

You can make any of the quilts in this book larger simply by making more blocks. Use the following mattress sizes as guidelines. These measurements include the top of the mattress only and do not include any overhang.

Baby	23" x 46"
Twin	39" x 75"
Double or Full	54" x 75"
Queen	60" x 80"
King	80" x 80"

Using any of the 10" blocks in this book, you need 3 x 4 blocks for a baby quilt (12 total), 4 x 6 blocks for a lap or youth quilt (24 total), 4 x 7 blocks for a twin (28 total), 5 x 7 for a double or full (35 total), 6 x 8 for a queen (48 total), and 8 x 8 (64 total) for a king. Add borders as needed to obtain the size you desire.

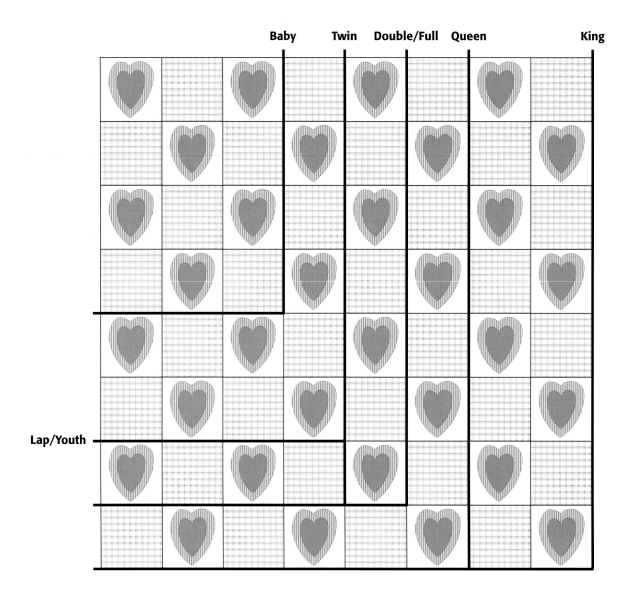

Tips and Tricks for Working with Flannels

- Clean your sewing machine often when you use flannel. The nap creates lint, and lots of it.

- Flannels shrink more per yard than regular cottons, so be sure to prewash flannels twice when getting ready to make a quilt.

- Because flannels are more stretchy than regular cottons, try a little spray sizing (available in the laundry detergent section of the grocery store) to slightly stiffen the fabric.

- Handle flannels carefully. Press gently, but firmly. Try not to stretch them. Expect that blocks won't look perfectly square no matter how careful you are. Cut pieces may not look square even right after you have cut them. Don't worry about this. Just as easily as they stretch out of shape, they can be eased back into shape when you sew the pieces together.

- Use the same-size sewing machine needles and same thread size that you would use with regular cottons. You don't need heavier thread or larger needles.

- Use a slightly longer stitch length when sewing flannel. A longer stitch length allows the nap enough room so that you can ease the flannel while stitching. With an American-made sewing machine, sew with 10 stitches per inch, rather than the usual 12. With a European-made machine, sew with a 3.0 stitch length, not the usual 2.5.

- Instead of a standard presser foot, consider using a walking foot when sewing flannels together. They will feed more evenly and shift less.

- Flannels may require easing as you sew. Even if you are very careful as you handle and sew flannels, you may find that the two pieces, although cut the same size, are slightly different when you are ready to sew them together. Align the edges and pin at the beginning and at the end of your stitching; then stretch slightly as you sew, easing the longer piece into the shorter one. I find that I ease flannel pieces together more often than I do regular cottons.

- Press seams to one side, or press them open to reduce bulk. It's up to you.

- Whoever said you can't combine flannels with nonflannels? Flannels and homespun-looking fabrics are naturals together. Both have a warm and cozy feel.

- The flannels for your quilt don't have to be newly purchased. You can find wonderful flannel shirts and pajamas in thrift shops, already washed for you! "Family Flannels" on page 31 includes fabrics from my family's outgrown flannel garments. What fun it is to look at it and see that "this block is from Ben's pajamas, that one is Mom's old dress."

- Don't bother to cut plaid and striped flannels on the lines. Cutting off-grain adds interest to the block and to the quilt, giving it a personality all its own. An exception to this is a large plaid or striped flannel used in borders. Cut off-grain, the long, bold lines in these flannels often take your attention away from the pieced or appliquéd blocks.

- Keep your pieced blocks simple. Because many flannels have interesting, often large, designs and lots of texture due to the nap, complex blocks are not required. The fabric does the design work for you. I prefer simple, traditional blocks when working with flannels.

- Use large blocks when making flannel quilts. Small blocks mean smaller pieces, and seam allowances can get very bulky. Most of the blocks in this book are 10" finished. If you want to make a flannel quilt using a favorite small block, enlarge the block size.

- Consider thinner battings for flannel quilts. The flannel itself is somewhat bulkier than regular cottons, due to the nap. Using a thinner batting makes a flannel quilt softer, more pliable, and more similar in weight to regular cotton quilts.

- Don't bind flannel quilts with flannel binding. Use a regular cotton homespun or other regular cotton fabric. Flannel bindings are bulky and can feel somewhat stiff, not soft.

Easing

The Patterns

The quilts in this book are meant to be idea starters. Many of the projects show a photo of a quilt as well as a block in another colorway. As you look at the quilts in this book, in shops, and at quilt shows, look beyond the colors you see. Look at the block. Look at the setting. You can use those ideas in your quilts and make them in any colors you want!

Making quilts should be fun. Try to enjoy the process as much as you expect to enjoy the product. Remember that we are not making quilts for the same reasons our grandmothers did. If we don't finish a quilt today, it doesn't mean we'll be cold tonight. We are making quilts to do something special for our families, our friends, or ourselves. Quilting should reduce stress, not induce it.

As you work, expect mistakes and try to see them as opportunities to create something better. When I make a mistake, I try to work with it. It's often the mistakes that I've corrected that give a quilt its uniqueness, its character. And sometimes, so-called mistakes aren't even noticeable to anyone but you, the maker of the quilt. Remember the "galloping horse" test. If you think a mistake is glaring, pin your block or your quilt top on a wall and pretend you're galloping by on a horse. Would you notice the mistake? If not, no one else will notice either. Leave it.

Always remember that quiltmaking is supposed to be fun!

Here are a few things to remember as you make the flannel quilts in this book.

- The yardage requirements for the quilts in this book are based on at least 40" of usable width after prewashing. If your fabric is narrower, you will probably need to cut more strips from additional yardage to get the required pieces. It's a good idea to check the fabric width before you cut and sew. An extra ¼ yard has been allowed for shrinkage, and sometimes more if a large amount is required. I'd rather you have too much than too little. You can use extra fabric to create a randomly pieced backing or to make pillows that coordinate with your quilt.

- Note that sometimes the sashing fabric and the first border fabric are listed separately in the Materials list. If you want to use the same fabric for both, add the two yardage amounts together. I like to use the same fabric for the sashing and inner border because it frames the blocks nicely.

- Prewash all your fabrics twice.

- Cut strips across the width of the fabric unless otherwise indicated.

- ◻ This symbol means to cut squares once diagonally.

- ⊠ This symbol means to cut squares twice diagonally.

- Make sure your seam allowances are ¼" wide. Aligning fabric edges with a standard presser foot usually creates a seam allowance that is too wide (see page 16).

- Pin to prevent shifting.

- Press seams after each step. Use steam for flatter seams. Pay attention to pressing arrows. If arrows aren't shown in the illustrations, the pressing direction doesn't matter.

- The cut sizes of side and corner triangles are larger than necessary. I prefer to trim a little fabric off rather than not have all that I need.

- Cutting dimensions are provided for border strips; however, it is always a good idea to measure your quilt top before adding borders (see page 87).

- Refer to "Finishing the Quilt" on pages 87–93 for directions on adding borders and finishing.

100 Squares *by Sandy Bonsib, 2000, Issaquah, Washington, 55½" x 55½"; machine quilted by Becky Kraus. This is a very quick and easy quilt. I arranged 100 squares randomly, distributing the dark and light squares evenly throughout the quilt. Just for fun, I embellished it with buttons after it was quilted.*

FABRIC	CUTTING
Materials: 40"-wide fabric	Measurements include ¼" seam allowances.
3¼ yds. total assorted red and blue plaid flannels in light, medium, and dark values	100 squares, 6" x 6"
3⅔ yds. for backing	
¾ yd. for bias binding	Enough 2"-wide bias strips to total at least 232" when joined
81 assorted red and blue buttons (optional)	

Directions

1. Arrange the squares in 10 rows of 10 squares each, distributing light, medium, and dark colors evenly throughout the quilt top. Sew the squares together in horizontal rows, alternating the pressing direction from row to row.

2. Join the rows.

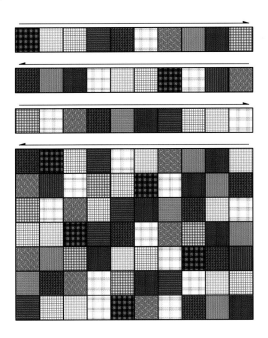

3. Layer the quilt top with batting and backing; baste. Quilt as desired. Bind the edges and label your quilt.

Optional: Stitch buttons at the corners where four squares meet. You can hide the knot between the button and the quilt top if you do not want it to show on the back of the quilt. You could also leave the knot and a short tail showing on top of the button, creating a surface embellishment. *Do not* add buttons if the quilt is intended for a small child.

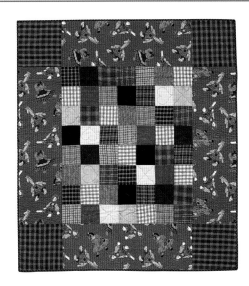

Alternate Quilt
Choose a juvenile novelty print, select fabrics to coordinate with it, and make a quick and easy child's quilt.

Blue-Work Babies *by Sandy Bonsib, 2000, Issaquah, Washington, 35¼" x 35¼"; machine quilted by Becky Kraus. I found these blue-work squares in a quilt shop. The Square Within a Square was the perfect block in which to feature them.*

FABRIC	CUTTING
Materials: 40"-wide fabric	Measurements include ¼" seam allowances.
4 blue-work-stitched squares*	6" x 6" (A)
½ yd. medium blue solid flannel for blocks	8 squares, 6" x 6"; ◻ to yield 16 triangles (B)
¾ yd. dark blue checked flannel for plain block and side and corner triangles	1 square, 9¼" x 9¼", for plain block (C) 1 square, 14" x 14"; ⊠ to yield 4 side triangles (D) 2 squares, 8½" x 8½"; ◻ to yield 4 corner triangles (E)
½ yd. dark blue solid flannel for inner border	28 rectangles, 2⅜" x 4¼" (F)
¾ yd. white solid flannel for inner and outer borders	60 squares, 2⅜" x 2⅜" (G), for inner border 2 strips, 2⅞" x 30½", for outer side borders 2 strips, 2⅞" x 35¼", for outer top/bottom borders
1¼ yds. for backing	
⅜ yd. for straight-grain binding	4 strips, 2" x 40"

*Purchase, or stitch red-work patterns in blue thread on 6" squares.

Directions

1. Sew 2 B triangles to opposite sides of an A square and trim as shown. Sew 2 more B triangles to the remaining sides of the square. Trim to 9¼" x 9¼". Make 4 total.

2. Referring to the color photo on page 28 and the diagram below, arrange the blocks, the C square, and 4 D triangles in diagonal rows. Sew the units together in diagonal rows. Join the rows, adding the E corner triangles last. Trim the quilt top to 26¾" x 26¾".

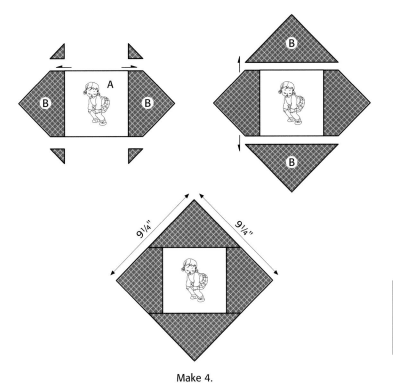

Make 4.

3. Referring to the "Sew and Flip" method on page 16, sew 2 G squares to an F rectangle. Make 28 units total.

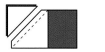

Make 28.

4. Sew 7 F/G units together to make each of 4 inner borders. Sew 2 of the inner borders to the sides of the quilt top. Add a G square to each end of the remaining inner borders, and sew these to the top and bottom edges.

5. Sew outer borders to the sides of the quilt top first; then add the borders to the top and bottom edges.

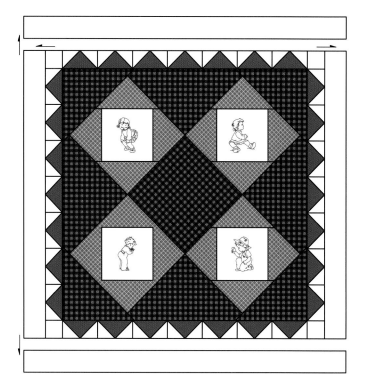

6. Layer the quilt top with batting and backing; baste. Quilt as desired. Bind the edges and label your quilt.

Quilting detail

Family Flannels *by Sandy Bonsib, 2000, Issaquah, Washington, 60½" x 70½"; machine quilted by Becky Kraus. This quilt made me feel like my grandmother must have felt when she made her quilts. I collected my family's outgrown flannel pajamas, boxers, shirts, dresses, and shorts. Then I cut them into large squares and stitched them together to form the quilt top. My good friend Kathy Staley stitched my favorite flannel nightgown, which I couldn't bear to cut up, onto the top by hand with pearl cotton. Notice how Kathy's blanket stitch shows off the collar and front placket. When my family members look at this, they talk about which squares came from their own clothing.*

FABRIC	CUTTING
Materials: 40"-wide fabric	Measurements include ¼" seam allowances.
Your favorite nightgown or pajamas	
2 yds. total assorted light-colored flannels*	18 squares, 10½" x 10½"
2⅜ yds. total assorted dark flannels*	20 squares, 10½" x 10½"
¾ yd. red plaid flannel	4 squares, 10½" x 10½"
Three 7" x 7" flannel squares for stars	3 of Template 1
4 yds. for backing (horizontal seam)	
1 yd. for bias binding	Enough 2"-wide bias strips to total at least 265" when joined
1 package of ½"-wide bias binding	2 pieces, 12" long, for bias stems
No. 5 pearl cotton to coordinate with fabric	
Size 20 chenille needle	

*Cut squares from pajamas, nightgowns, boxer shorts, dresses, and shirts.

Directions

1. Referring to the photograph on page 31 and the diagram at right, arrange the light and dark squares into 7 rows of 6 blocks each. Sew the squares together in horizontal rows. Join the rows.

2. Place your favorite nightgown or pajamas on the quilt top. Arrange as desired. Pin; then stitch in place with pearl cotton. Add additional stitching, if desired, such as buttonhole stitching around the collar and down the front placket.

3. Referring to the color photo on page 31, appliqué the stars and bias stems in place.

4. Layer the quilt top with batting and backing; baste. Quilt as desired. Don't forget to quilt inside your favorite garment. Bind the edges and label your quilt.

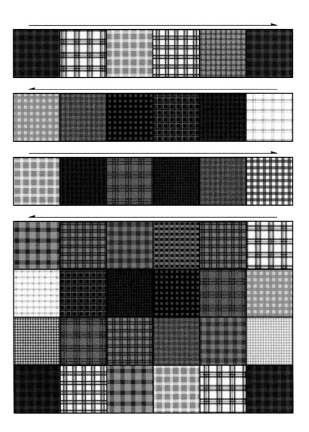

Stitching detail

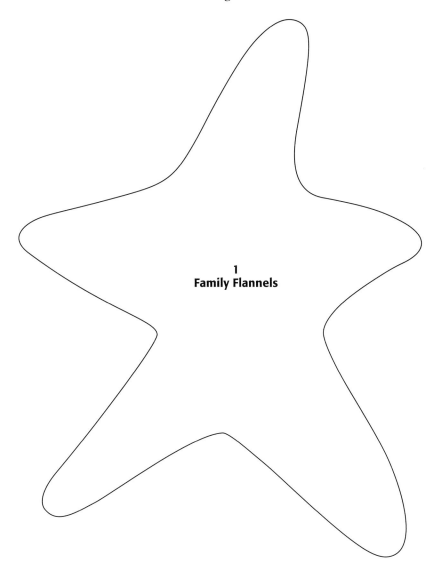

1
Family Flannels

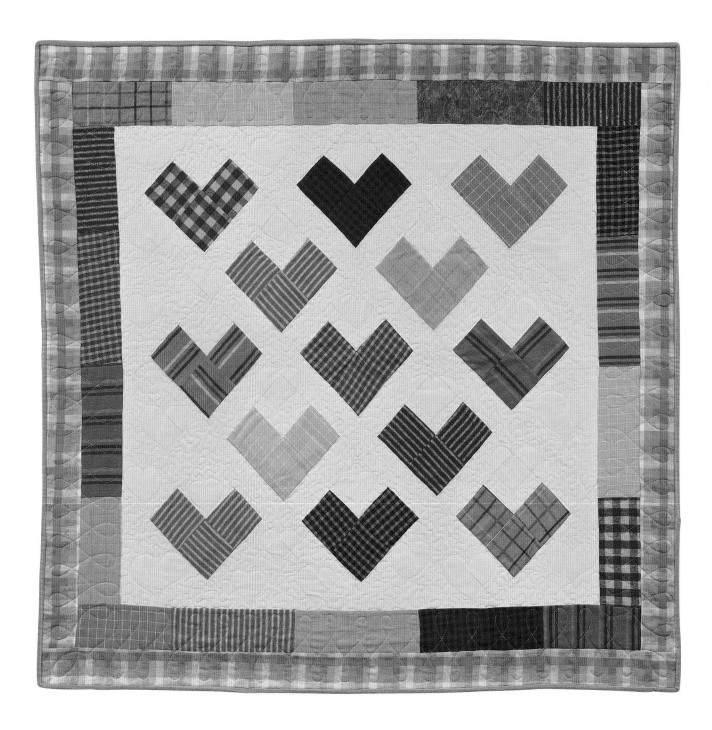

Easy Four Patch Hearts *by Sandy Bonsib, 2000, Issaquah, Washington, 47" x 47";
machine quilted by Becky Kraus. Many quilters love hearts, and I am no exception. I've
made hearts many different ways, some more complex than others. This was the simplest heart I've ever made: just 3 colored squares and a background square to form a
Four Patch block, which looks like a heart when set on-point.*

FABRIC	CUTTING
Materials: 40"-wide fabric	Measurements include ¼" seam allowance.
13 fat eighths (9" x 20") in assorted striped and plaid flannels for blocks and inner border	From each fat eighth, cut: 3 squares, 3½" x 3½", for blocks From the remaining fabrics, cut: 18 rectangles, 3½" x 9½", for inner border
1⅔ yds. yellow solid flannel for blocks, sashing, and side and corner triangles	13 squares, 3½" x 3½", for blocks 8 rectangles, 2½" x 6½", for sashing 2 strips, 2½" x 38½", for sashing 2 strips, 2½" x 22½", for sashing 2 squares, 15" x 15", ⊠ to yield 8 side triangles 2 squares, 10" x 10", ◻ to yield 4 corner triangles
½ yd. plaid flannel for outer border	5 strips, 3" x 40"
3 yds. for backing	
⅜ yd. for straight-grain binding	5 strips, 2" x 40"

Directions

1. Sew together 3 matching 3½" heart-fabric squares and 1 yellow 3½" background square to make a Four Patch block. Make 13 total.

Make 13.

2. Referring to the color photo on page 34 and the diagram at right, arrange the blocks and 6½"-long sashing strips in diagonal rows. Sew the blocks and sashing strips together. Sew a 38½"-long sashing strip to both sides of the 5-block row. Sew a 22½"-long sashing strip to 1 side of each 3-block row. Sew the side triangles to the ends of each row, including the single blocks. Join the rows, adding the corner triangles last.

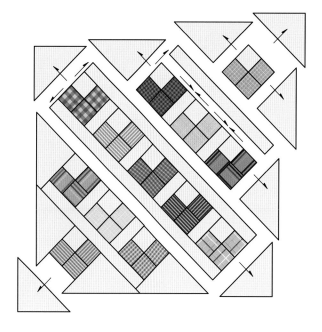

3. Trim the quilt top 2¼" from the points of the hearts. You'll be trimming more off the top edge than the other 3 edges.

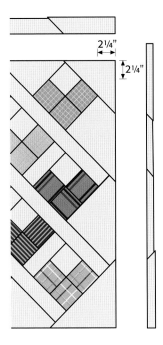

6. Layer the quilt top with batting and backing; baste. Quilt as desired. Bind the edges and label your quilt.

Quilting detail

4. Referring to the color photo on page 34, arrange the 3½" x 9½" inner border rectangles around the quilt top with 4 rectangles on each side, and 5 each on the top and bottom. Position the rectangles so that they are not near hearts of the same color. Sew the side rectangles together end to end. Trim to 36" and add to the sides of the quilt top. Sew the top and bottom rectangles together end to end. Trim to 42" and add to the top and bottom edges.

5. Sew the 3"-wide outer border strips together end to end. From this strip, cut 2 pieces, 42" long, for the side borders, and 2 pieces, 47" long, for the top and bottom borders. Sew the borders to the sides of the quilt top first; then add the borders to the top and bottom edges.

Alternate Block
Choose pastels for your hearts to make a special quilt for baby.

Hearts in the Garden *by Sandy Bonsib, 2000, Issaquah, Washington, 55½" x 55½"; machine quilted by Becky Kraus. This quilt features assorted fabrics from In The Beginning Fabrics.*

FABRIC	CUTTING
Materials: 40"-wide fabric	Measurements include ¼" seam allowances.
1 yd. floral flannel	9 of Template 2
1 yd. pink solid flannel for blocks	5 squares, 10½" x 10½" (A) 16 rectangles, 1½" x 10½" (B) 20 squares, 1½" x 1½" (C)
1 yd. yellow solid flannel for blocks and middle border	4 squares, 10½" x 10½" (A) 20 rectangles, 1½" x 10½" (B) 16 squares, 1½" x 1½" (C) 5 strips, 2" x 40", for middle border
¼ yd. each pink, blue, and green checked flannels for inner border	2 strips of each color, 2½" x 40" (6 total) 4 blue check squares, 2½" x 2½"
½ yd. each pink, blue, green, and violet print flannels for outer border	1 strip of each color; 6½" x 40" (4 total) 1 rectangle of each color, 5" x 6½" (4 total)
¼ yd. yellow checked flannel for corner squares	4 squares, 6½" x 6½"
3½ yds. for backing	
½ yd. for straight-grain binding	6 strips, 2" x 40"

Directions

1. Referring to "Appliqué" on pages 18–19, appliqué the hearts to the pink and yellow A squares. I used needle-turn appliqué because the flannel turns under easily and holds a crease well.

2. To the pink A squares, sew 4 yellow B rectangles and 4 pink C squares as shown. To the yellow A squares, sew 4 pink B rectangles and 4 yellow C squares as shown.

3. Referring to the color photo on page 37, arrange the pink and yellow blocks in 3 rows of 3 blocks each, alternating the background colors. Sew the blocks together in horizontal rows. Join the rows.

4. Sew together 1 each of the pink, blue, and green 2½"-wide strips to make a strip set. Make 2 strip sets. From the strip sets, cut 24 segments, each 2½" wide.

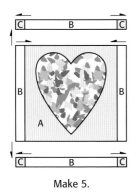

Make 5.

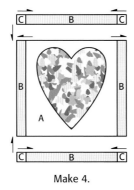

Make 4.

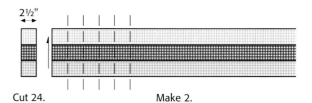

2½"

Cut 24.   Make 2.

5. Sew together 6 segments to make each of 4 inner borders. Sew the borders to the sides of the quilt top. Sew a blue check square to each end of the remaining borders and add these to the top and bottom edges.

8. Layer the quilt top with batting and backing; baste. Quilt as desired. Bind the edges and label your quilt.

Quilting detail

6. Sew the 2"-wide yellow middle border strips together end to end. From this strip, cut 2 strips, 40½" long, for the side borders and 2 strips, 43½" long, for the top and bottom borders. Sew the borders to the sides of the quilt top first; then add the borders to the top and bottom edges.

7. Sew each of the 6½" x 40" strips to a matching 5" x 6½" rectangle, joining the 6½" edges. From each joined strip, cut 1 piece, 43½" long, for the outer borders. Arrange borders as desired on each side of the quilt. Sew borders to the sides of the quilt top first. Sew a 6½" yellow check corner square to each end of the remaining borders; then add these borders to the top and bottom edges.

Alternate Block
Try richly colored solids for your heart blocks.

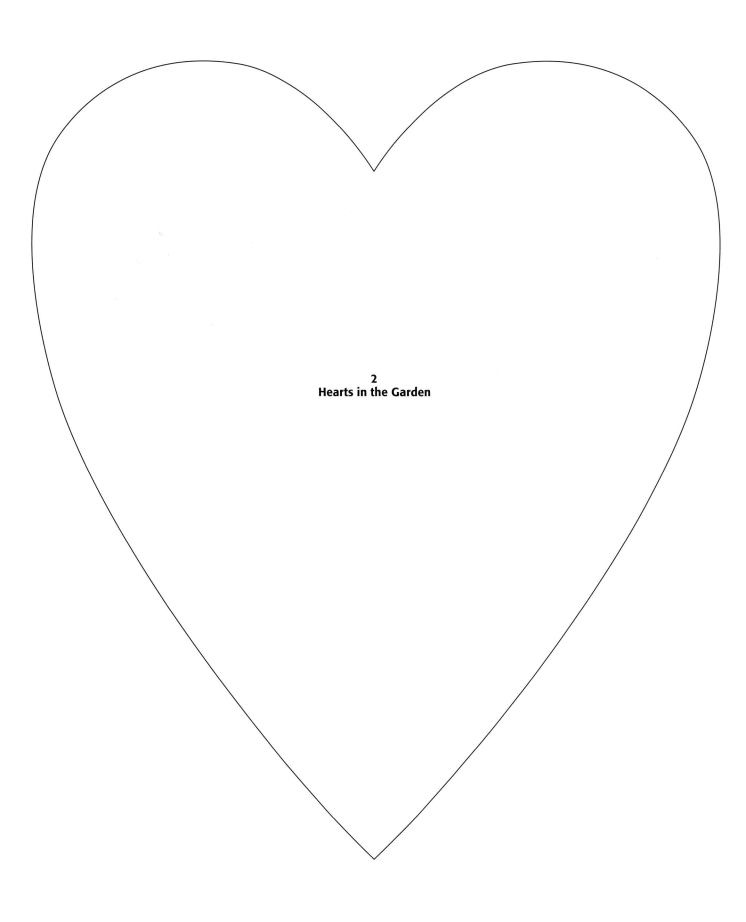

2
Hearts in the Garden

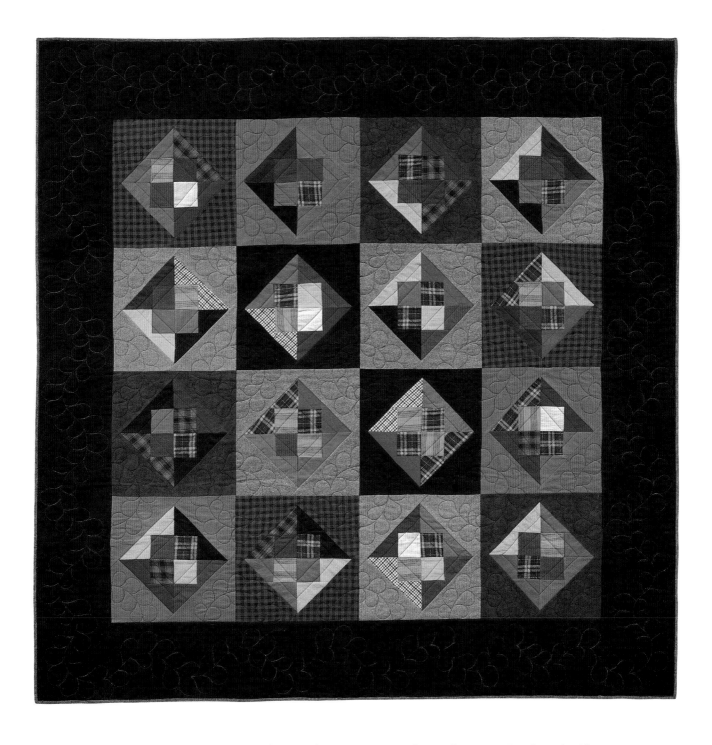

Almost Amish *by Sandy Bonsib, 2000, Issaquah, Washington, 67½" x 67½"; machine quilted by Becky Kraus. This quilt began with simple Square Within a Square blocks. I wanted to do something special with them, so I cut them into quarters and combined four quarters to make new blocks. Because of the many solid flannels, including black, this quilt has an almost Amish look to it, hence its name.*

FABRIC	CUTTING
Materials: 40"-wide fabric	Measurements include ¼" seam allowances.
¼ yd. each of 8 assorted plaid, print, and solid flannels in black, blue, and red	6 squares, 6" x 6", from each print (48 total); ◻ 32 of the squares to yield 64 triangles (B). (You will need 16 sets of 4 matching triangles.). You will have 16 squares left over for block centers (A).
⅔ yd. each of 6 assorted flannels	32 squares, 8½" x 8½"; ◻ to yield 64 triangles (C). You will need 16 sets of 4 matching triangles.
2 yds. black flannel for border	7 strips, 8½" x 40"
4⅜ yds. for backing	
½ yd. for straight-grain binding	7 strips, 2" x 40"

Directions

1. Using 4 matching B triangles, sew 2 to opposite sides of an A square and trim as shown. Sew 2 more to the remaining sides of the square to complete the Square Within a Square block. Make 16 total.

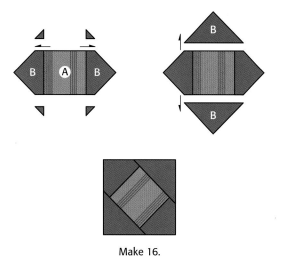

Make 16.

2. Cut the blocks from corner to corner on both diagonals. Join 4 different quarters to create a new block. Make 16 total. Trim the blocks to 8½" x 8½".

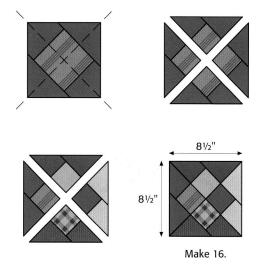

8½"

8½"

Make 16.

3. Using 4 matching C triangles, sew 2 to opposite sides of a block created in step 2; trim as shown in step 1. Sew 2 more to the remaining sides of the block. Make 16 total. Trim the blocks to 13¼" x 13¼".

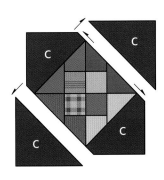

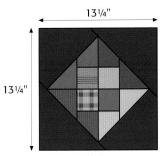

13¼"

13¼"

Make 16.

4. Arrange the blocks in 4 rows of 4 blocks each. Sew the blocks together in horizontal rows. Join the rows.

5. Sew the 8½"-wide border strips together end to end. From this strip, cut 2 strips, 51½" long, for the side borders, and 2 strips, 67½" long, for the top and bottom borders. Sew borders to the sides of the quilt top first; then add borders to the top and bottom edges.

6. Layer the quilt top with batting and backing; baste. Quilt as desired. Bind the edges and label your quilt.

Quilting detail

Playful Puppies

Playful Puppies *by Sandy Bonsib, 2000, Issaquah, Washington, 56½" x 62½"; machine quilted by Becky Kraus. I love animals and am currently raising a guide-dog puppy, Dermot, for Guide Dogs for the Blind. He does so many funny things every day that make me laugh. This quilt, with the puppies' ears stitched down in all directions, reminds me of his many antics.*

FABRIC	CUTTING
Materials: 40"-wide fabric	Measurements include ¼" seam allowances.
⅝ yd. each of 6 assorted plaids, prints, and solids for blocks and cornerstones	9 rectangles, 8½" x 10½" (A) 18 and 18 reversed of Template 3. You will need 4 matching ears for each dog. 4 squares, 3" x 3" (E), for cornerstones *For each rectangle A, cut the following background pieces from matching fabric:* 2 squares, 2⅞" x 2⅞" (B) 2 rectangles, 3" x 8½" (C) 2 rectangles, 3" x 15½" (D)
1¾ yds. of black for sashing and borders	6 rectangles, 3" x 15½" (F), for vertical sashing 6 rectangles, 3" x 13½" (G), for horizontal sashing 6 strips, 6½" x 40", for borders
3⅝ yds. for backing (horizontal seam)	
½ yd. for straight-grain binding	7 strips, 2" x 40"
No. 8 pearl cotton in black, gold, and white	
Size 24 chenille needle	
18 medium buttons for eyes	
9 large buttons for noses	

Directions

1. Referring to the "Sew and Flip" method on page 16, sew 2 matching B squares to the bottom of each A rectangle.

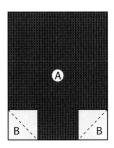
Stitch.

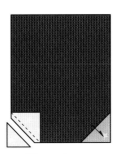
Trim and press.

2. Referring to the photograph on page 44 and mouth pattern on page 47, stitch the face details with a double strand of pearl cotton. Be sure to use a thread color that contrasts with the face fabric.

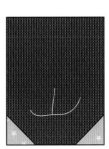

3. Use 4 matching ear pieces to create 2 ears. Pair 2 ear pieces, with right sides together. Sew around the curved edge, leaving the straight edge open. Turn the ears right side out and press. Make 9 pairs of ears total.

Stitch, leaving top open.

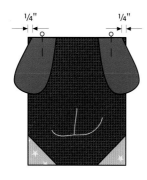

Turn and press.
Make 9 pairs.

4. Place the ears at the top of the face, ¼" in from the side edges. Pin in place.

5. Using C and D rectangles to match the B squares, sew the C rectangles to the top and bottom edges first; then sew the D rectangles to the sides. If necessary, pin the ears out of the way so you do not catch them in your seams. Press the seams toward the C and D rectangles.

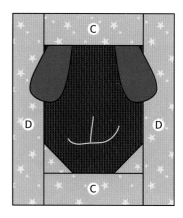

6. Referring to the color photo on page 44 and the diagram below, arrange and sew the blocks and vertical sashing strips (F) in 3 horizontal rows. Sew together 3 G sashing strips and 2 E squares to make each of 2 sashing rows. Join the rows of blocks and sashing rows.

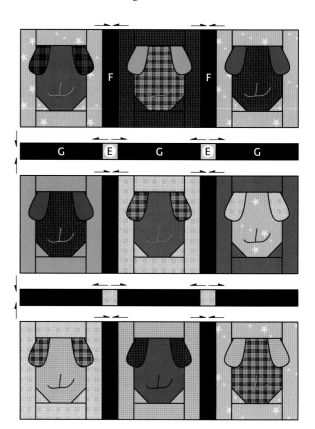

7. Sew the 6½"-wide black border strips together end to end. From this strip, cut 2 strips, 50½" long, for the side borders, and 2 strips, 56½" long, for the top and bottom borders. Sew the borders to the sides of the quilt top first, then to the top and bottom edges.

8. Layer the quilt top with batting and backing; baste. Quilt as desired. Bind the edges and label your quilt. Stitch medium buttons for eyes and large buttons for noses. If desired, hide the knots between the buttons and the quilt top. Referring to the photo, tack down the ears in a variety of positions to show how playful your pups are!

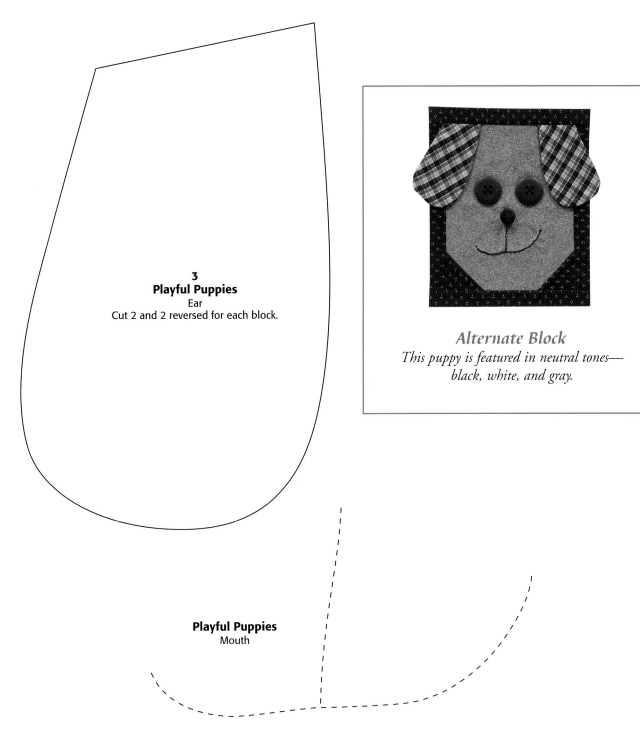

3
Playful Puppies
Ear
Cut 2 and 2 reversed for each block.

Alternate Block
This puppy is featured in neutral tones—black, white, and gray.

Playful Puppies
Mouth

Wear Your Shades, Baby!
This Quilt Is Bright!

Wear Your Shades, Baby! This Quilt Is Bright! *By Sandy Bonsib, 2000, Issaquah, Washington, 66" x 78½"; machine quilted by Becky Kraus. This quilt was inspired by Freddy Moran. In her book* Freddy's House, *she said that she considers the color red a neutral, so I decided to play with using red as a background fabric in this quilt. I don't think I've ever made a brighter quilt. Don't try to sleep under this one!*

FABRIC	CUTTING
Materials: 40"-wide fabric	Measurements include ¼" seam allowances.
¼ yd. orange striped flannel	4 squares, 5½" x 5½" 4 squares, 3" x 3"
¼ yd. yellow-and-orange checked flannel	6 squares, 5½" x 5½" 6 squares, 3" x 3"
¼ yd. light blue plaid flannel	6 squares, 5½" x 5½" 6 squares, 3" x 3"
¼ yd. dark blue plaid flannel	6 squares, 5½" x 5½" 6 squares, 3" x 3"
¼ yd. green checked flannel	8 squares, 5½" x 5½" 8 squares, 3" x 3"
¼ yd. purple plaid flannel	10 squares, 5½" x 5½" 10 squares, 3" x 3"
4 yds. red solid flannel for background, sashing, and borders	40 squares, 5½" x 5½", for background 15 rectangles, 3" x 10½", for vertical sashing 5 strips, 3" x 40", for horizontal sashing 7 strips, 9½" x 40", for borders
4¼ yds. for backing (horizontal seam)	
⅝ yd. for straight-grain binding.	8 strips, 2" x 40"

Directions

1. Referring to the "Sew and Flip" method on page 16, sew a 3" square to a red 5½" square. The total number of units needed is listed in the caption below.

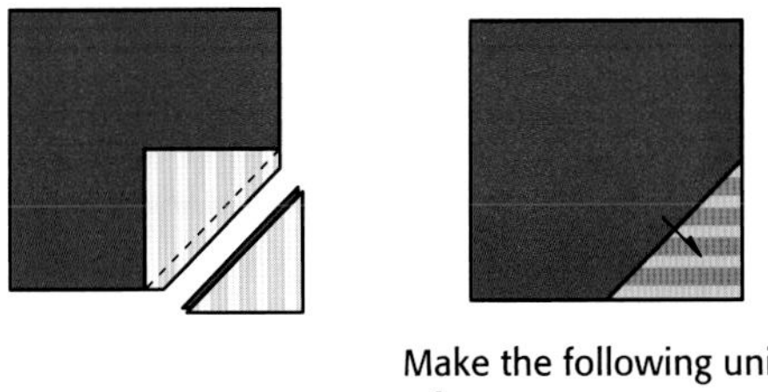

Make the following units:
4 orange
6 yellow-and-orange
6 light blue
6 dark blue
8 green
10 purple

2. Sew 2 matching units made in step 1 together with 2 matching 5½" squares to make a Bow Tie block. Make 2 orange blocks, 3 yellow-and-orange blocks, 3 light blue blocks, 3 dark blue blocks, 4 green blocks, and 5 purple blocks.

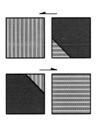

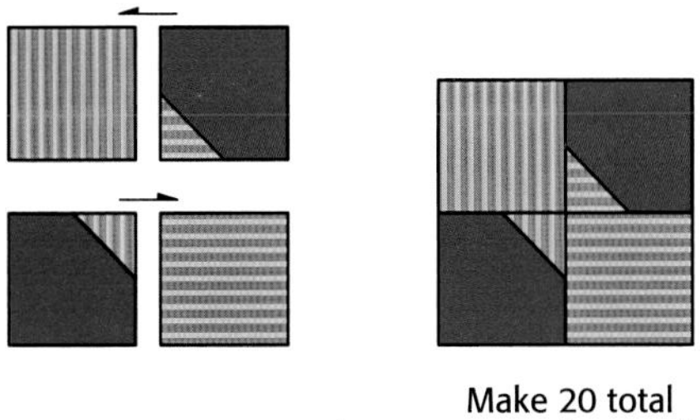

Make 20 total
(2 orange, 3 yellow-and-orange,
3 light blue, 3 dark blue,
4 green, 5 purple).

3. Referring to the color photo on page 48 and the diagram below, arrange and sew the blocks and vertical sashing strips in 5 horizontal rows, with 4 blocks in each row.

4. Sew the red 3"-wide horizontal sashing strips together end to end. From this strip, cut 4 strips, 48" long. Join the rows of blocks and sashing strips.

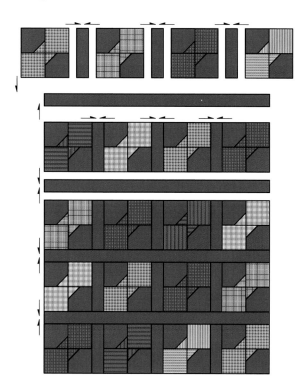

5. Sew the red 9½"-wide border strips together end to end. From this strip, cut 2 strips, 60½" long, for the side borders, and 2 strips, 66" long, for the top and bottom borders. Sew borders to the sides of the quilt top first; then add borders to the top and bottom edges.

6. Layer the quilt top with batting and backing; baste. Quilt as desired. Bind the edges and label your quilt.

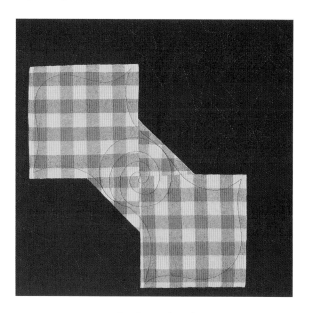

Quilting detail

Alternate Block
Wonderful florals, in large- and medium-scale prints, make attractive Bow Tie blocks.

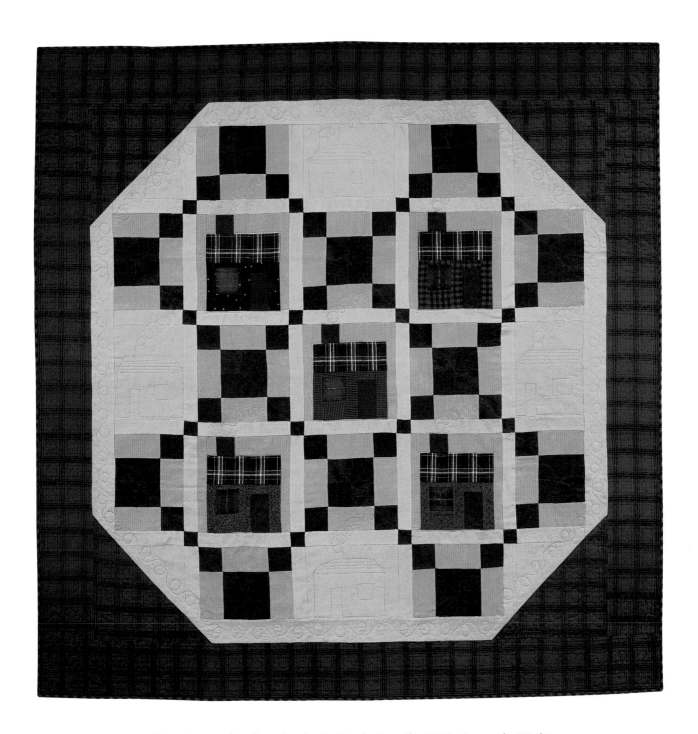

Hot Chocolate and a Storybook *by Sandy Bonsib, 2000, Issaquah, Washington, 68½" x 68½"; machine quilted by Becky Kraus. The House block is one of my favorites. I created this block from only squares and rectangles, even the roof, making it easier to piece than a more traditional house with a triangular roof. I named this quilt when my daughter Kate told me it looked like a quilt you should snuggle under on a cold winter day with hot chocolate and a storybook.*

FABRIC	CUTTING
Materials: 40"-wide fabric	Measurements include ¼" seam allowances.
⅛ yd. navy blue plaid flannel for roofs	5 pieces, 3½" x 8½" (D)
¼ yd. navy blue solid flannel for chimneys and doors	5 pieces, 2½" x 2½" (B) 5 pieces, 2½" x 4½" (I)
⅛ yd. blue plaid flannel for windows	5 pieces, 3" x 3" (F)
⅛ yd. each of 5 red flannels for house fronts	1 strip, 2½" x 40", from each red flannel (5 total)
	From each strip, cut the following: 1 piece, 1" x 3" (E) 1 piece, 2½" x 3" (G) 1 piece, 1½" x 2½" (H) 1 piece, 1½" x 5½" (J) 2 pieces, 1¾" x 5½" (K)
⅞ yd. tan #1 flannel for houses and alternate blocks	5 pieces, 1½" x 2½" (A) 5 pieces, 2½" x 5½" (C) 10 pieces, 1½" x 10½" (L) 24 rectangles, 3" x 5½", for alternate blocks 1 strip, 5½" x 40", for alternate blocks 1 strip, 5½" x 12", for alternate blocks
½ yd. red solid flannel for alternate blocks	3 strips, 3" x 40" 1 strip, 3" x 12"
½ yd. navy blue solid flannel for alternate blocks	3 strips, 3" x 40" 1 strip, 3" x 12"
2¼ yds. tan #2 flannel for sashing, side rectangles, corner squares, and inner border	24 rectangles, 2" x 10½", for sashing 16 rectangles, 2" x 8", for sashing 4 rectangles, 8" x 10½", for side rectangles 4 squares, 8" x 8", for corner squares 6 strips, 3" x 40", for inner border
⅛ yd. red solid flannel for cornerstones	8 squares, 2" x 2"
⅛ yd. navy blue solid flannel for cornerstones	8 squares 2" x 2"
2¼ yds. red-and-navy blue plaid flannel for corner triangles and outer border	4 squares, 13½" x 13½" 7 strips, 6½" x 40"
4¼ yds. for backing	
1 yd. for bias binding	Enough 2"-wide bias strips to total at least 284" when joined

Directions

1. Sew together pieces A–L as shown to make a House block. Make 5 total. For piece F, you might want to choose a plaid that mimics the look of windowpanes, as shown below.

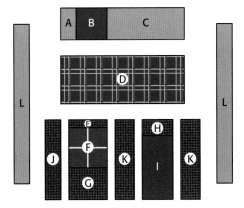

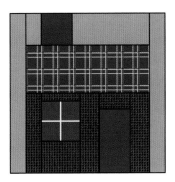

Make 5.

2. Sew a 3" x 40" red strip to a 3" x 40" navy blue strip to make a strip set. Make 2 strip sets. From the strip sets, cut 24 segments, 3" wide.

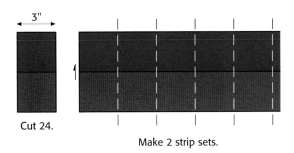

Cut 24.

Make 2 strip sets.

3. Sew 2 segments together to make a four-patch unit, making sure to reverse 1 of the segments. Make 12 total.

Make 12.

4. Sew a 3" x 40" red strip and a 3" x 40" navy blue strip to opposite sides of a 5½" x 40" tan #1 strip to make a strip set. Repeat with the 12"-long red, navy blue, and tan #1 strips to make a second strip set. From the strip sets, cut 16 segments, 3" wide.

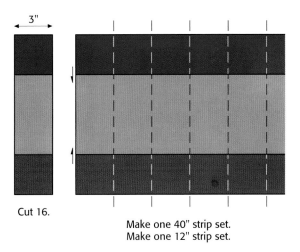

Cut 16.

Make one 40" strip set.
Make one 12" strip set.

5. Sew together 1 four-patch unit, two 3" x 5½" tan #1 rectangles, and 2 segments from step 4 to make an alternate block. Position the segments from step 4 so that the red and blue squares form a diagonal line. Make 4 total.

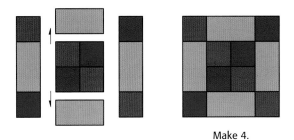

Make 4.

6. Sew 1 four-patch unit, two 3" x 5½" tan #1 rectangles, and 1 segment from step 4 together to make each of 4 alternate partial units for the sides. Repeat to make each of 4 alternate partial units for the top and bottom edges. Notice the position of the red and blue squares.

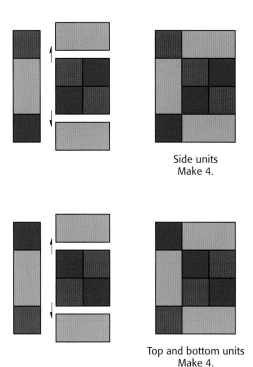

Side units
Make 4.

Top and bottom units
Make 4.

7. Referring to the color photo on page 51 and the diagram on page 55, arrange the House blocks, alternate blocks, alternate partial blocks, sashing strips, cornerstones, side rectangles, and corner squares in horizontal rows. Sew the blocks and sashing strips together. Sew the sashing strips and cornerstones together to make sashing rows. Join the rows of blocks and sashing rows.

8. Referring to the "Sew and Flip" method on page 16, mark the diagonal on the wrong side of each 13½" red-and-navy blue plaid square. Place 1 square at each corner of the quilt top, right sides together. Sew on the diagonal line, flip, press, and trim the back 2 layers.

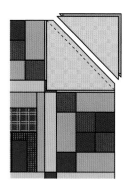 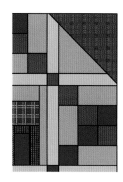

9. Sew the 3"-wide tan #2 inner border strips together end to end. From this strip, cut 2 strips, 51½" long, for the side borders, and 2 strips, 56½" long, for the top and bottom borders. Sew the borders to the sides of the quilt top first; then sew the borders to the top and bottom edges.

10. Sew the 6½"-wide red-and-navy blue plaid outer border strips together end to end. From this strip, cut 2 strips, 56½" long, for the side borders, and 2 strips, 68½" long, for the top and bottom borders. Sew the borders to the sides first; then add the borders to the top and bottom edges.

11. Layer the quilt top with batting and backing; baste. Quilt as desired—you might want to quilt houses in the plain squares, as shown below. Bind the edges and label your quilt.

Quilting detail

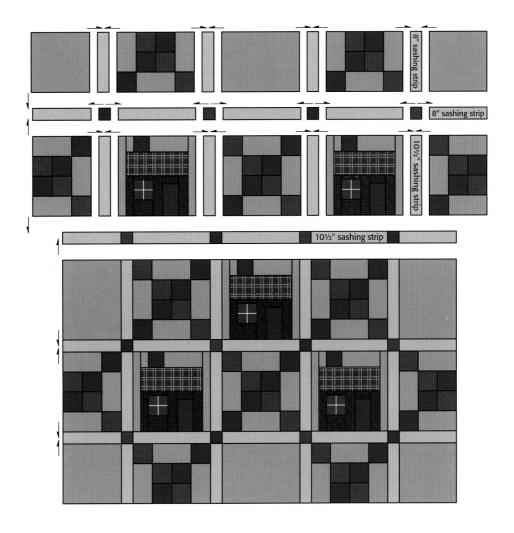

8" sashing strip

8" sashing strip

10½" sashing strip

10½" sashing strip

10½" sashing strip

Alternate Block
For a different look, use a large-scale floral
print for the roofs of your houses.

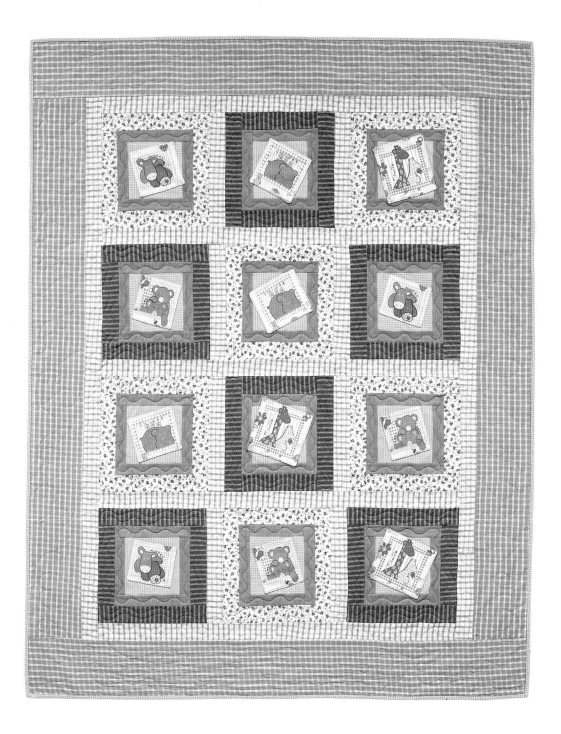

Baby Animals for Baby *by Sandy Bonsib, 2000, Issaquah, Washington, 46½" x 58";
machine quilted by Becky Kraus. A flannel with a baby print inspired me to cut up
and feature these motifs in the centers of Courthouse Step blocks. For the border, I
wanted to use more of the motif fabric but discovered that it was too busy, so I chose
another border fabric instead. The animal motifs were appliquéd to the block centers
with yellow pearl cotton.*

FABRIC	CUTTING
Materials: 40"-wide fabric	Measurements include ¼" seam allowances.
1 yd. novelty print flannel	12 motifs*
½ yd. yellow checked flannel	12 squares, 5½" x 5½" (A)
⅔ yd. blue solid flannel	24 rectangles, 1½" x 5½" (B) 24 rectangles, 1½" x 7½" (C)
½ yd. blue striped flannel	12 rectangles, 2" x 7½" (D) 12 rectangles, 2" x 10½" (E)
½ yd. floral flannel	12 rectangles, 2" x 7½" (F) 12 rectangles, 2" x 10½" (G)
¾ yd. white-and-pink plaid flannel for sashing and inner border	8 rectangles, 2" x 10½", for vertical sashing 3 strips, 2" x 33½", for horizontal sashing 5 strips, 2" x 40", for inner borders
1¼ yds. pink-and-white plaid flannel for outer border	6 strips, 5½" x 40"
3 yds. for backing (horizontal seam)	
½ yd. for straight-grain binding	6 strips, 2" x 40"
No. 8 yellow pearl cotton	
Size 24 chenille needle	

*Center the motifs, and cut squares or rectangles around them. (See "Fussy Cutting" on page 11.)

Directions

1. Sew pieces A–E in alphabetical order to make a Courthouse Steps block. Make 6 blocks in each of 2 different fabric combinations (12 total).

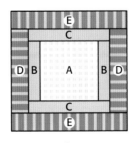

Make 6.

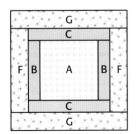

Make 6.

2. Turn under the ¼" seam allowances on the edges of the motifs and press. Arrange them on the center of each block, placing them askew so that some tilt to the left, others to the right. Stitch them in place with pearl cotton and a running stitch.

3. Referring to the color photo on page 56 and the diagram below, arrange the blocks and vertical sashing strips together in 4 horizontal rows. Alternate the block combinations from row to row. Sew the blocks and sashing strips together. Join the rows with horizontal sashing strips between the rows.

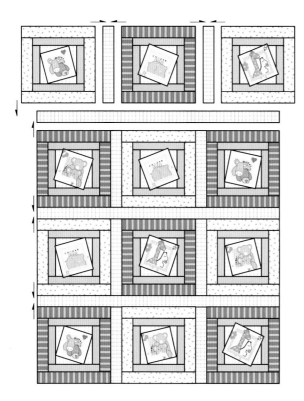

4. Sew the 2" x 40" inner border strips together end to end. From this strip, cut 2 strips, 45" long, for the side borders, and 2 strips, 2" x 36½", for the top and bottom borders. Sew borders to the sides of the quilt top first; then add borders to the top and bottom edges.

5. Sew the 5½"-wide outer border strips together end to end. From this strip, cut 2 strips, 48" long, for the side borders and 2 strips, 46½" long, for the top and bottom borders. Sew the borders to the sides first; then add borders to the top and bottom edges.

6. Layer the quilt top with batting and backing; baste. Quilt as desired. Bind the edges and label your quilt.

Quilting detail

Alternate Block
Fussy cut 5½" squares from a novelty print, centering the motifs, and piece them into the blocks. Then you won't have to do any appliqué.

Dynamic Duo: Plaid and Floral Stars *by Sandy Bonsib, 2000, Issaquah, Washington, 54½" x 54½"; machine quilted by Becky Kraus. My friend Trish Carey inspired me to make a quilt using plaids (which I love) and florals (which she loves, and which I don't usually use). I was surprised and dazzled by the result!*

FABRIC	CUTTING
Materials: 40"-wide fabric	Measurements include ¼" seam allowances.
¼ yd. each of 13 bright plaid and 13 bright floral flannels	For each block, select 1 plaid and 1 floral. Pick 1 fabric for the star and 1 for the background, and cut the following: 8 squares, 3" x 3", for star points (A) 4 rectangles, 3" x 5½", for background (B) 1 square, 5½" x 5½", for star center (C) 4 squares, 3" x 3", for background (D)
1 yd. blue-and-green plaid flannel for corner and side triangles	2 squares, 17" x 17"; ⊠ to yield 8 side triangles 2 squares, 10" x 10"; ◻ to yield 4 corner triangles
1¼ yds. blue plaid flannel for border	6 strips, 5½" x 40"
3½ yds. for backing	
½ yd. for straight-grain binding	6 strips, 2" x 40"

Directions

1. Referring to the "Sew and Flip" method on page 16, sew 2 A squares to a B rectangle to make a star-point unit. Make 4 units for each block.

2. Sew 2 D squares to each end of a star-point unit. Sew 2 star-point units to opposite sides of a C square. Join the units to complete a block. Make 13 blocks total.

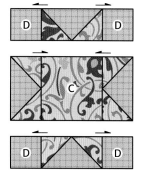
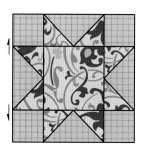

Make 13.

3. Referring to the color photo on page 59 and the diagram below, arrange and sew the blocks and side triangles in diagonal rows. Join the rows, adding the corner triangles last.

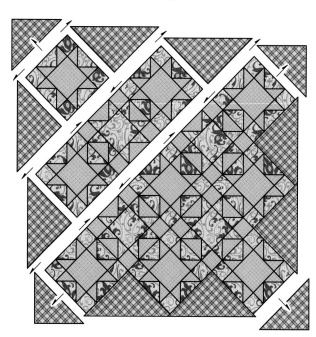

4. Trim the sides of the quilt top 1" from the block points.

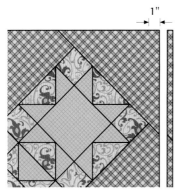

5. Sew the 5½"-wide border strips together end to end. From this strip, cut 2 strips, 44½" long, for the side borders and 2 strips, 54½" long, for the top and bottom borders. Sew the borders to the sides of the quilt top first; then add borders to the top and bottom edges.

6. Layer the quilt top with batting and backing; baste. Quilt as desired. Bind the edges and label your quilt.

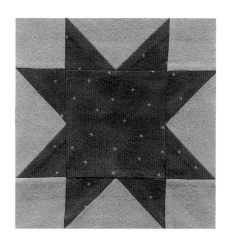

Alternate Block
This star looks marvelous in a rich gold and brown combination.

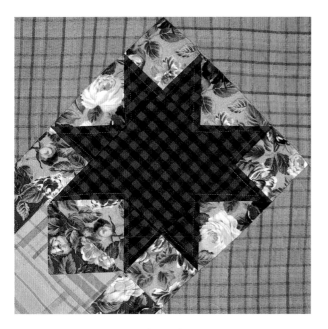

Quilting detail

Folk Flowers *by Sandy Bonsib, 2000, Issaquah, Washington, 53" x 73"; machine quilted by Becky Kraus. My love of folk art and a note card featuring a single flower inspired the simple flowers in this quilt. I used corner triangles to make this block a more interesting shape than just a rectangle.*

FABRIC	CUTTING
Materials: 40"-wide fabric	Measurements include ¼" seam allowances.
⅜ yd. each of 4 dark blue flannels for background and stems	12 rectangles, 10½" x 12½", for background 3 strips, 1⅞" x 40", for stems
Scraps of assorted orange flannel for flowers	12 rectangles, 7½" x 12"
⅝ yd. orange flannel for block corner triangles	48 squares, 3½" x 3½"
1¼ yds. orange plaid flannel for sashing and inner border	8 rectangles, 2½" x 12½", for vertical sashing 9 rectangles, 2½" x 10½", for horizontal sashing 6 strips, 3" x 40", for inner border
⅛ yd. red flannel for cornerstones	6 squares, 2½" x 2½"
1½ yds. dark orange plaid flannel for outer border	6 strips, 7¼" x 40"
3⅔ yds. for backing (horizontal seam)	
½ yd. for straight-grain binding	7 strips, 2" x 40"
No. 8 dark blue pearl cotton	
Size 24 chenille needle	

Directions

1. For flower stems, sew each 1⅞"-wide dark blue strip, *wrong sides together,* along the long edge with a ⅛"-wide seam. Press strips flat, centering the seam on the underside. Cut 12 strips, each 7" long.

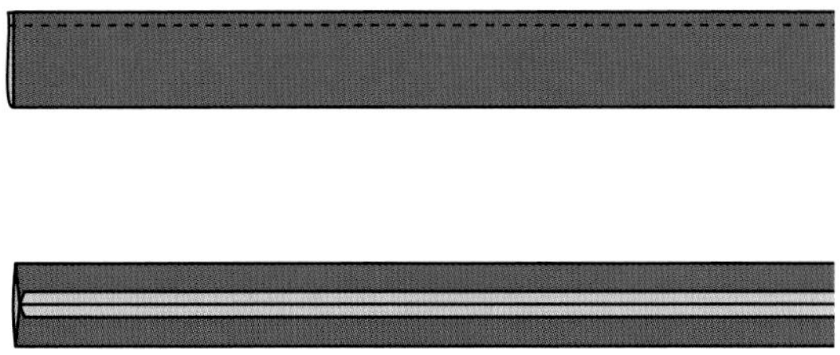

2. Referring to "Pocket Appliqué" on page 18 and using the 7½" x 12" orange rectangles, prepare 12 flowers.

3. Center the stem on the background rectangle. Add the flower, covering the top of the stem; pin in place. Although my stems are straight, I tilted some of the flowers to add interest. Using pearl cotton, stitch the stems along both sides with a running stitch, and stitch the flowers with a blanket stitch. Make 12 blocks total.

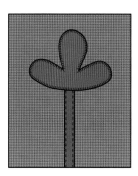

Make 12.

4. Referring to the "Sew and Flip" method on page 16, sew a 3½" orange square to each corner of the blocks. Trim the back 2 layers.

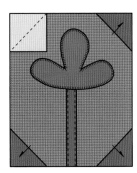

5. Referring to the color photo on page 62 and the diagram below, arrange and sew the blocks and 12½"-long vertical sashing strips into 4 horizontal rows. Join 3 of the 10½"-long horizontal sashing strips and 2 cornerstones to make each of 3 sashing rows. Join the rows of blocks and sashing rows.

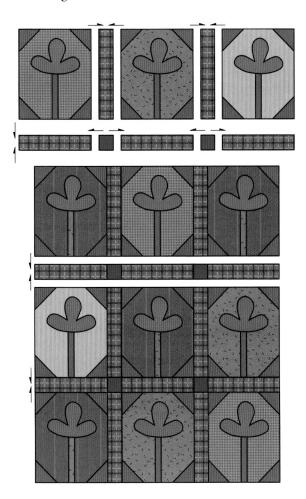

6. Sew the 3"-wide inner border strips together end to end. From this strip, cut 2 strips, 54½" long, for the side borders, and 2 strips, 39½" long, for the top and bottom borders. Sew borders to the sides of the quilt top first; then add borders to the top and bottom edges.

7. Sew the 7¼"-wide outer border strips together end to end. From this strip, cut 2 strips, 59½" long, for the side borders and 2 strips, 53" long, for the top and bottom borders. Sew the borders to the sides first; then add borders to the top and bottom edges.

8. Layer the quilt top with batting and backing; baste. Quilt as desired. For the borders, you might want to use a floral quilting pattern, as shown below, to complement the blocks. Bind the edges and label your quilt.

Quilting detail

Quilting detail

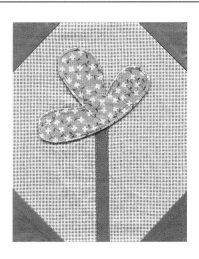

Alternate Block
Subtle pastels give this flower a soft appeal.

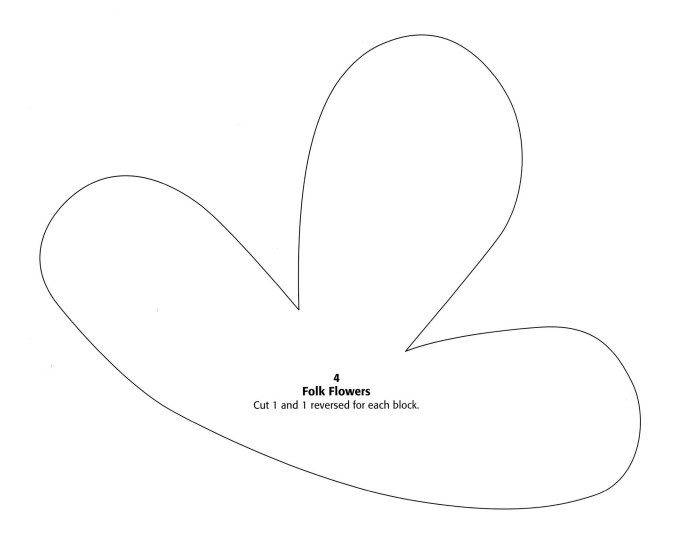

4
Folk Flowers
Cut 1 and 1 reversed for each block.

Color! Color! Color! *by Sandy Bonsib, 2000, Issaquah, Washington, 60½" x 60½";*
machine quilted by Becky Kraus. As a quilter without formal art training, I have
found the study of color and how colors interact quite interesting. This quilt loosely
represents a color wheel, starting with reds at the top, then, going clockwise, orange,
yellow, green, blue, and purple. Because I wanted to use many different colors in this
quilt, I needed to add a square or two of nonflannel fabric here and there to add to the
somewhat limited range of flannel colors I was able to find.

FABRIC	CUTTING
Materials: 40"-wide fabric	Measurements include ¼" seam allowances.
2½ yds. total flannels in assorted colors and values for blocks and outer border	32 squares, 6" x 6", for blocks 44 squares, 5½" x 5½", for outer border
1¾ yds. black flannel for blocks and inner checkerboard border	32 squares, 6" x 6" 6 strips, 3" x 40"
⅔ yd. white flannel for inner checkerboard border	6 strips, 3" x 40"
3¾ yds. for backing	
½ yd. for straight-grain binding	7 strips, 2" x 40"

Directions

1. Referring to the "Two for One" method on page 17, sew a 6" colored square and a 6" black square together to make 2 half-square-triangle blocks. Trim the blocks to 5½" x 5½". Repeat with the remaining 6" squares to make a total of 64 blocks.

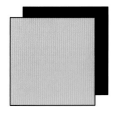

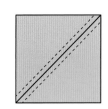

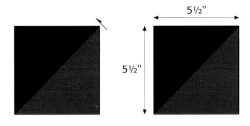

Make 64.

2. Referring to the color photo on page 66 and the diagram below, arrange the blocks into 8 rows of 8 blocks each, creating radiating bands of color from the center out. For example, place reds at the top of the quilt; then, proceeding clockwise, add the orange, yellow, green, blue, and purple blocks. Mix some colors with adjoining colors. For example, place 1 or 2 orange blocks in the red area and 1 or 2 in the yellow area. Do this for each color family.

3. Sew the blocks together in horizontal rows. Join the rows.

4. Sew 1 white 3"-wide strip to 1 black 3"-wide strip to make a strip set. Make 6 strip sets. From the strip sets, cut 72 segments, each 3" wide.

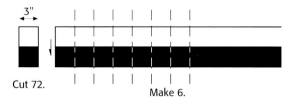

Cut 72.

Make 6.

5. Alternating the position of the black and white squares to form a checkerboard, sew 16 segments together to make each of the side borders. Sew these to opposite sides of the quilt top. Sew 20 segments together to make each of the top and bottom borders. Sew these to the top and bottom edges. Be sure the black and white squares alternate in the corners.

Side borders
Make 2.

Top and bottom borders
Make 2.

6. Referring again to the quilt photo, arrange the 5½" outer border squares around the outer edges of the quilt top. I tried to place the squares opposite their color family in the quilt top. Don't agonize over this. Sew 10 squares together to make each of the side borders. Sew these to opposite sides of the quilt top. Sew 12 squares together to make each of the top and bottom borders, and add these to the top and bottom edges.

7. Layer the quilt top with batting and backing; baste. Quilt as desired. Bind the edges and label your quilt.

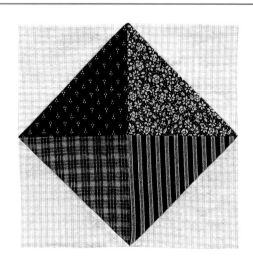

Alternate Block
By choosing neutral colors and arranging the half-square triangle blocks to form a diamond in the center, you can create a very different block.

Plaid Nine Patch *by Sandy Bonsib, 2000, Issaquah, Washington, 45" x 62"; machine quilted by Becky Kraus. My friend Margy Duncan created the Gingersnap Nine Patch pattern that inspired this quilt. I love Nine Patch blocks, plaids, and Margy's unique Nine Patch quilts in particular. With Margy's permission to use this pattern, I combined them all into this lively, colorful quilt.*

FABRIC	CUTTING
Materials: 40"-wide fabric	Measurements include ¼" seam allowances.
1 fat quarter each of 2 flannels for 3 center Nine Patch blocks	3 strips from each of 2 fabrics, 2½" x 20" (6 total)
½ yd. flannel for round 1 (8 plain blocks)	8 squares, 6½" x 6½"
2 fat quarters each of 2 flannels for round 2 (12 Nine Patch blocks)	9 strips from each of 2 fabrics, 2½" x 20" (18 total)
⅔ yd. flannel for round 3 (16 plain blocks)	16 squares, 6½" x 6½"
3 fat quarters each of 2 flannels for round 4 (20 Nine Patch blocks)	15 strips from each of 2 fabrics, 2½" x 20" (30 total)
¾ yd. plaid flannel for side and corner triangles	5 squares, 11" x 11"; ⊠ to yield 20 side triangles 2 squares, 8" x 8"; ◻ to yield 4 corner triangles
3 yds. for backing (horizontal seam)	
½ yd. for straight-grain binding	6 strips, 2" x 40"

Directions

The Nine Patch blocks and plain blocks are arranged in 4 rounds that surround the 3 vertical blocks in the center. Rounds 1 and 3 are plain blocks; rounds 2 and 4 are Nine Patch blocks.

Note: If you run out of a fabric, as I sometimes did, substitute another that is similar in color to the one you ran out of.

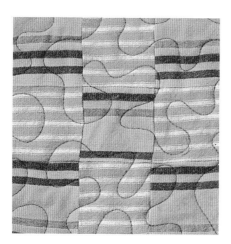

Nine Patch block

1. For each round of Nine Patch blocks, sew the 2½" x 20" strips together to make 2 different strip sets. From the strip sets, cut 2½"-wide segments as indicated.

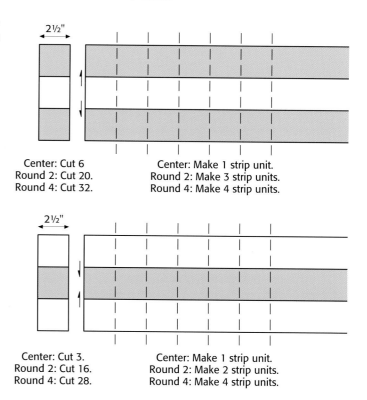

Center: Cut 6
Round 2: Cut 20.
Round 4: Cut 32.

Center: Make 1 strip unit.
Round 2: Make 3 strip units.
Round 4: Make 4 strip units.

Center: Cut 3.
Round 2: Cut 16.
Round 4: Cut 28.

Center: Make 1 strip unit.
Round 2: Make 2 strip units.
Round 4: Make 4 strip units.

2. Sew 3 segments together to make a Nine Patch block. Make blocks for each round as shown.

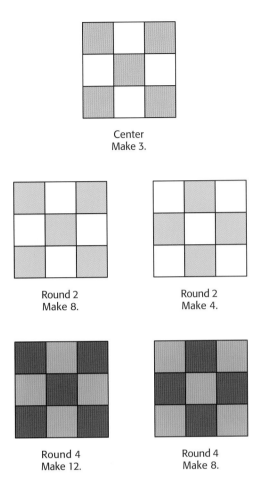

Center
Make 3.

Round 2
Make 8.

Round 2
Make 4.

Round 4
Make 12.

Round 4
Make 8.

Notice that some of the Nine Patch blocks have the darker fabric in the corners and the center; others have the lighter fabric in the corners and the center.

3. Referring to the color photo on page 69 and the diagram at right (top), arrange the rounds of plain blocks and Nine Patch blocks around the 3 center Nine Patch blocks. Add the side triangles along the outer edges. Sew the blocks and triangles together in diagonal rows. Press the seams toward the plain blocks and side triangles. Join the rows, adding the corner triangles last.

Trim the edges of the quilt top 1" from the block points.

Trim
to 1".

4. Layer the quilt top with batting and backing; baste. Quilt as desired. Bind the edges and label your quilt.

Alternate Block
Use red and green for a Christmas Nine Patch quilt.

Old-Fashioned Baskets *by Sandy Bonsib, 2000, Issaquah, Washington, 55¾" x 55¾"; machine quilted by Becky Kraus. Years ago, Roberta Horton helped me see the beauty of Basket blocks. These blocks are present in many antique quilts. The Cake Stand blocks are featured with alternating squares and side and corner triangles that are a nonflannel floral fabric. The neutral colors give the quilt a soft, older look.*

FABRIC	CUTTING
Materials: 40"-wide fabric	Measurements include ¼" seam allowances.
9 fat quarters of assorted white, gray, and black flannels for blocks	For each basket, cut: 3 squares, 3⅜" x 3⅜", from basket fabric (A) ◹ 3 squares, 3⅜" x 3⅜", from background fabric (A) ◹ 1 square, 5⅞" x 5⅞", from basket fabric (B) ◹ (You will only use 1.) 1 square, 5⅞" x 5⅞", from background fabric (B) ◹ (You will only use 1.) 2 squares, 3" x 3" (C) 2 rectangles, 3" x 5½" (D)
1½ yds. white-and-gray print for plain blocks and side and corner triangles	4 squares, 10½" x 10½", for plain blocks 2 squares, 18" x 18"; ⊠ to yield 8 side triangles 2 squares, 12" x 12"; ◻ to yield 4 corner triangles
¼ yd. black flannel for inner border	5 strips, 1¼" x 40"
1 yd. gray flannel for outer border	6 strips, 5" x 40"
3¾ yds. for backing	
½ yd. for straight-grain binding	7 strips, 2" x 40"

Directions

1. For each basket, sew the A basket triangles to the A background triangles. Make 6 matching half-square-triangle units. Sew a B basket triangle to a B background triangle. Make 1 large unit to match the 6 smaller units.

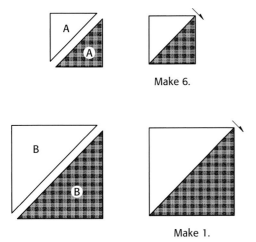

Make 6.

Make 1.

2. Arrange and sew together the triangle units, the matching C squares, and the matching D rectangles for the background.

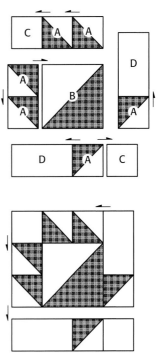

Make 9.

3. Repeat steps 1 and 2 to make 9 blocks.

4. Referring to the color photo on page 72 and the diagram below, arrange the Basket blocks, plain blocks, and side triangles in diagonal rows. Sew the units together. Join the rows, adding the corner triangles last.

5. Trim the edges of the quilt top to 1⅜" from the points of the Basket blocks.

6. Sew the 1¼"-wide inner border strips together end to end. From this strip, cut 2 pieces, 45¼" long, for the side borders and 2 pieces, 46¾" long, for the top and bottom borders. Sew borders to the sides of the quilt top first; then add borders to the top and bottom edges.

7. Sew the 5"-wide outer border strips together end to end. From this strip, cut 2 pieces, 46¾" long, for the side borders and 2 pieces, 55¾" long, for the top and bottom borders. Sew the borders to the sides first, then to the top and bottom edges.

8. Layer the quilt top with batting and backing; baste. Quilt as desired. Bind the edges and label your quilt.

Quilting detail

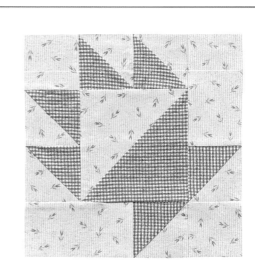

Alternate Block
Yellow and blue pastels give a springlike look and feel to this basket.

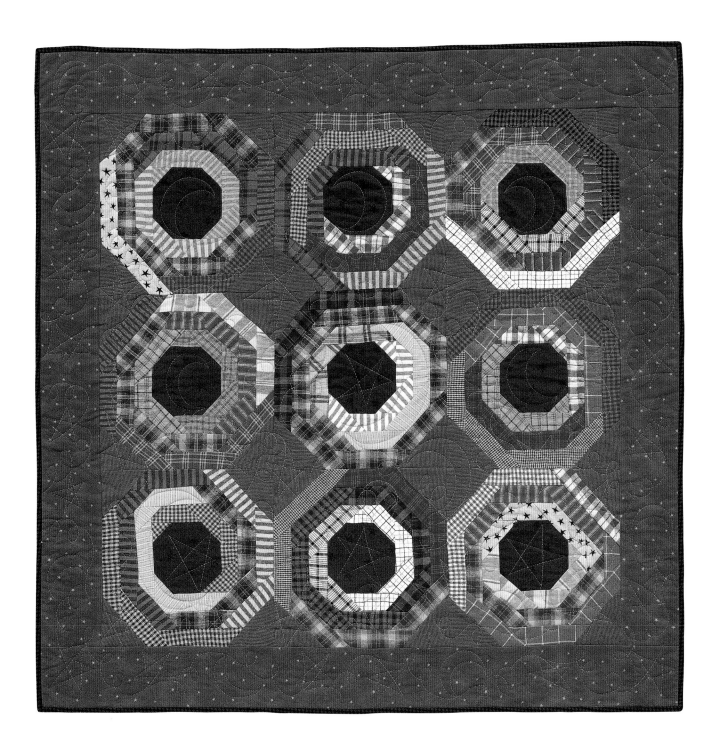

Circle Around *by Sandy Bonsib, 2000, Issaquah, Washington, 37½" x 37½"; machine quilted by Becky Kraus. This quilt was inspired by a picture of a hooked rug. I started with a square center, trimmed it to an octagon, and began adding strips, log-cabin style, to create circle blocks without curved piecing. By adding triangles to the corners of each block, I made squares that were easy to piece together.*

FABRIC	CUTTING
Materials: 40"-wide fabric	Measurements include ¼" seam allowances.
¼ yd. dark red flannel print for centers	9 of Template 5
32 fat eighths (9" x 20") of assorted flannel prints	2 strips from each, 1½" x 20" (64 total)
⅜ yd. blue flannel for corner triangles	18 squares, 4" x 4"; ◻ to yield 36 triangles
⅝ yd. brown flannel print for borders	2 strips, 4" x 30½", for side borders 2 strips, 4" x 37½", for top and bottom borders
1½ yds. for backing	
⅜ yd. for straight-grain binding	4 strips, 2" x 40"

Directions

1. For each block, sew a 1½"-wide strip to 1 edge of a red octagon. Press the seam toward the strip and trim the excess even with the sides of the octagon. Working clockwise, sew the same-color strip to each side of the octagon, trimming after each strip is added. Use a single 20"-long strip until it is used up; then begin a new strip.

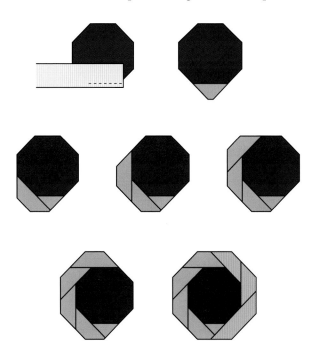

2. Continue adding strips until you have 3 rounds of strips on all sides of the red octagon.

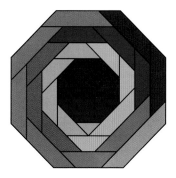

3. Sew a blue triangle to each corner of the block to form a square.

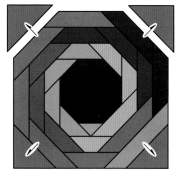

Make 9.

4. Referring to the color photo on page 75, arrange the blocks in 3 rows of 3 blocks each. Rotate the blocks one-quarter turn as often as desired until you have a satisfactory balance of colors and fabrics. Sew the blocks together in horizontal rows. Join the rows.

5. Sew the 4" x 30½" border strips to the sides of the quilt top. Sew the 4" x 37½" strips to the top and bottom edges.

6. Layer the quilt top with batting and backing; baste. Quilt as desired. Bind the edges and label your quilt.

Alternate Block
Blue and white fabric arranged to form rings around the center hexagon, which features a "fussy cut" floral motif, create a block that looks very different from the original.

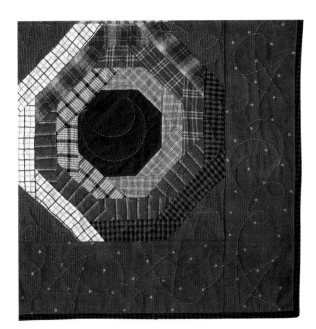

Quilting detail

5
Circle Around

Opposite: Flannel Sampler *by Sandy Bonsib, 2000, Issaquah, Washington, 50½" x 73¼"; machine quilted by Becky Kraus. A sampler quilt is one that includes many different block designs in a single quilt. Sampler quilts first appeared in the United States in the mid-1800s. Initially, many sampler quilts were appliquéd, but as appliqué fell out of fashion, quiltmakers made more pieced-block samplers, especially after 1875.*

Samplers were sometimes called "pattern quilts" and were made to record a quiltmaker's file of designs. In addition, each block could also be used for drawing templates. Many different sampler blocks, in varying degrees of difficulty, showed off a young woman's sewing skill.

This sampler includes eight 10" blocks. By adding additional 10" blocks or repeating some blocks, this sampler can be enlarged to fit any size bed or wall.

FABRIC	CUTTING
Materials: 40"-wide fabric	Measurements include ¼" seam allowances.
20 to 25 fat eighths and fat quarters in assorted red, white, and blue flannels	See instructions for making individual blocks for cutting directions.
⅓ yd. of 8 red, white, and blue flannels for triangles around blocks*	2 squares, 10" x 10", from each fabric (16 total); ◻ to yield 32 triangles
⅔ yd *each* of 2 red flannels for sashing	12 rectangles, 2½" x 14½", from each fabric (24 total)
⅛ yd. blue checked flannel for cornerstones	17 squares, 2½" x 2½"
2⅛ yds. blue plaid flannel for side and corner triangles	2 squares, 26" x 26"; ⊠ to yield 8 side triangles (you will use only 6) 2 squares, 16" x 16"; ◻ to yield 4 corner triangles
3⅜ yds. for backing (horizontal seam)	
⅝ yd. for straight-grain binding	8 strips, 2" x 40"

*If you want the large triangles to match the block background, be sure to purchase fabrics to match. Triangles don't need to match the background of the blocks; it's up to you.

Basket

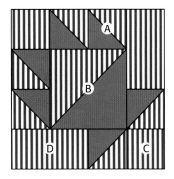

A (Basket): 3 squares, 3⅜" x 3⅜" ◻

B (Basket): 1 square, 5⅞" x 5⅞" ◻ (Use only 1)

A (Background): 3 squares, 3⅜" x 3⅜" ◻

B (Background): 1 square, 5⅞" x 5⅞" ◻
 (Use only 1)

C (Background): 2 squares, 3" x 3"

D (Background): 2 rectangles, 3" x 5½"

Refer to directions on page 73 to make the block.

Star

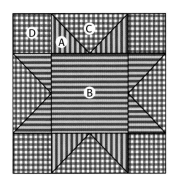

A (Star): 8 squares, 3" x 3"

B (Star): 1 square, 5½" x 5½"

C (Background): 4 rectangles, 3" x 5½"

D (Background): 4 squares, 3" x 3"

Refer to directions on page 60 to make the block.

Puppy

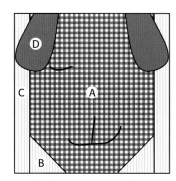

A (Puppy's face): 1 rectangle, 8½" x 10½"

B (Background): 2 squares, 2⅞" x 2⅞"

C (Background): 2 rectangles, 1½" x 10½"

Ears: 2 and 2 reversed of Template 3 (page 47)

2 large buttons

No. 5 pearl cotton

Size 20 chenille needle

Refer to directions on pages 45–46 to make the block. There are no strips added to the top and bottom of the block. Stitch the winking eye, the line below where the nose will be, and the mouth. Add the buttons for the eye and nose after you finish the quilting.

Circle Around

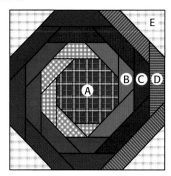

A: 1 of Template 5 (page 77)

B: 1 strip, 1½" x 40"

C: 1 strip, 1½" x 40"

D: 1 strip, 1½" x 40"

E: 2 squares, 4" x 4"; ◻

Refer to directions on page 76 to make the block. Use the same fabric for each complete round that surrounds the center octagon.

House

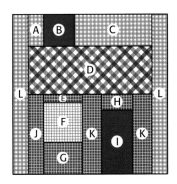

A (Background): 1 rectangle, 1½" x 2½"

B (Chimney): 1 square, 2½" x 2½"

C (Background): 1 rectangle, 2½" x 5½"

D (Roof): 1 rectangle, 3½" x 8½"

E (House): 1 rectangle, 1" x 3"

F (Window): 1 square, 3" x 3"

G (House): 1 rectangle, 2½" x 3"

H (House): 1 rectangle, 1½" x 2½"

I (Door): 1 rectangle, 2½" x 4½"

J (House): 1 rectangle, 1½" x 5½"

K (House): 2 rectangles, 1¾" x 5½"

L (Background): 2 rectangles, 1½" x 10½"

Refer to directions on page 53 to make the block.

Bow Tie

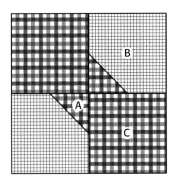

A (Bow tie): 2 squares, 3" x 3"

B (Bow tie): 2 squares, 5½" x 5½"

C (Background): 2 squares, 5½" x 5½"

Refer to directions on page 49 to make the block.

Folk Flower

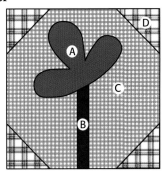

A: 1 of Template 4 (page 65)

B (Stem): 1 rectangle, 1⅞" x 6"

C (Background): 1 square, 10½" x 10½"

D (Corner triangles): 4 squares, 3½" x 3½"

Refer to directions on pages 63–64 to make the block.

Note: This block is square in the sampler quilt.

Folk Heart

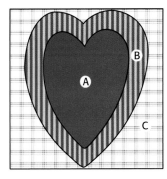

A (Small heart): 1 of Template 6 (page 84)

B (Large heart): 1 of Template 7 (page 84)

C (Background): 1 square, 10½" x 10½"

Appliqué the large heart to the background square. Appliqué the smaller heart inside the larger one.

Assembling the Quilt

1. Sew 2 matching large triangles to opposite sides of each block, and trim as shown. Add matching triangles to remaining sides of the block. If you prefer, do not use matching triangles around the blocks. Trim the block to 14½" x 14½", centering the block. Repeat for each block.

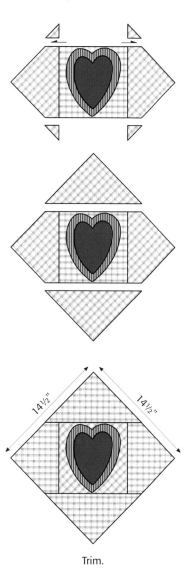

Trim.

2. Referring to the color photo on page 78 and the diagram below, arrange the blocks, sashing strips, cornerstones, and side triangles in diagonal rows. Sew the blocks and sashing strips together. Sew the sashing strips and cornerstones together to make sashing rows. Join the rows of blocks and sashing rows, adding the side triangles as shown. Join all the rows, adding the corner triangles last.

3. Trim the quilt top 1¼" from the points of the cornerstones.

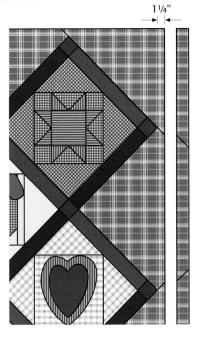

1¼"

4. Layer the quilt top with batting and backing; baste. Quilt as desired. Bind the edges and label your quilt.

Sampler Class

Samplers are often used as a teaching tool. In a quilting class, a student can learn a variety of techniques by making different blocks. An example of how to teach this quilt in six class sessions might be:

Class 1: Discuss tips and tricks for working with flannel. Show how to make the following blocks:
- *House* (squares and rectangles)
- *Bow Tie* (sew-and-flip technique)

Class 2: Show how to make the following blocks:
- *Puppy* (sew and flip, making ears, backstitching with pearl cotton)
- *Star* (sew-and-flip variation)

Class 3: Show how to make the following blocks:
- *Heart* (appliqué)
- *Folk Flower* (appliqué, making stems)

Class 4: Have students bring previously made blocks to this class so you can help them choose fabric for sashing, posts, and side and corner triangles. They can then prewash these fabrics and bring them to Class 5. Show how to make the following blocks:
- *Basket* (half-square triangles)
- *Circle Around* (Log Cabin variation)

Class 5: Demonstrate adding triangles to the blocks, choosing and cutting sashing strips and cornerstones, and adding side and corner triangles.

Class 6: Demonstrate hand or machine quilting. If hand quilting, try using No. 8 pearl cotton for larger, more primitive stitches, or No. 12 for smaller stitches. Demonstrate binding. Create a label, perhaps having everyone in class sign each other's label.

This class could be adapted to more sessions, teaching only one block per session and allowing more sewing time, or fewer sessions if more sewing time is available or if students sew at home. Most importantly, students will have fun learning different blocks and different techniques for working with flannels.

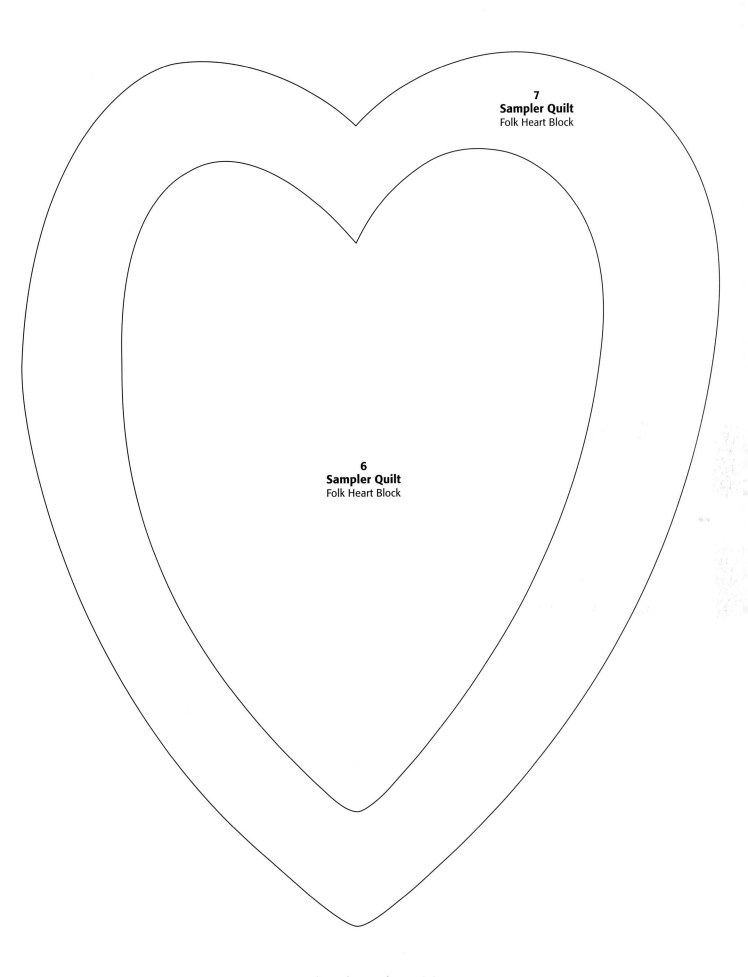

7
Sampler Quilt
Folk Heart Block

6
Sampler Quilt
Folk Heart Block

Finishing the Quilt

Adding Borders

You will see borders with and without corner squares on the quilts in this book. Some quilts don't even have borders. Borders are not an absolute requirement. If you like your quilt without them, eliminate them. If you want to make your quilt larger, especially to fit a bed, adding additional borders or making borders wider than the pattern specifies can easily accomplish that.

The most fabric-efficient way to cut borders is on the crosswise grain, which means across the width of the fabric. Since many quilts are longer than a piece of fabric cut on the crosswise grain, you may need to piece two or more strips together to create one long enough for the edge of your quilt. When piecing border strips, I prefer to use a diagonal seam.

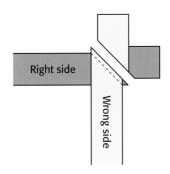

With flannel quilts, I prefer to cut borders along the lengthwise grain because flannel stretches less than standard quiltmaking cottons. Despite my preference, I usually cut flannel borders along the crosswise grain because it's much more fabric-efficient for a non-directional print.

A directional print is one in which the motifs (trees, children, snowmen) all face the same direction. If you want the design to face the same direction in all the borders, you'll need to cut two borders from the crosswise grain and two borders from the

lengthwise grain. If you want to cut your directional-print borders this way, or if you prefer to cut even non-directional borders from the lengthwise grain, you'll need to purchase more fabric for your border. You will need enough for the longest length of your quilt and then some. For example, if a quilt measures 55" x 75", I purchase 84" (2⅓ yds.) of fabric. This allows me to cut my long borders without piecing them and also allows for shrinkage, which could be 4" to 6" with this length of fabric.

Directional border prints pose a different set of problems. If you want the design in a directional print to face the same direction in all the borders, you need to cut two borders from the crosswise grain and two borders from the lengthwise grain. To do this, you will need to purchase extra fabric. For 8"-wide borders on a quilt that measures 55" x 75", you need to have 75" for the side borders, plus 24" to piece the top and bottom borders (3 strips x 8"); 75" + 24" = 99" or 2¾ yards. Adding extra for shrinkage, I would buy at least 3 yards, or to be safe, 3¼ yards.

It's important to measure and cut border strips to fit your quilt. Cutting strips and sewing them to the quilt top without measuring often results in a quilt with wavy borders. The edges of a quilt may be slightly longer than the measurement through the center due to stretching during construction. This is normal, so it's important to measure through the center of the quilt, not along the edges.

Specific measurements are provided for cutting the border strips for each quilt. These measurements are based on blocks sewn with accurate ¼"-wide seam allowances. Measure your blocks to be sure they are the correct size. To be safe, measure your quilt top after the blocks are sewn together to determine the correct border lengths.

Borders without Corner Squares

Many of the projects in this book do not use corner squares. If the quilt directions call for corner squares and you prefer not to use them, be sure to add extra yardage to the border strips before you cut.

1. Measure the length of the quilt top through the center. Cut 2 borders strips to that measurement. Mark the center of the quilt edges and the border strips with a pin. You can also mark quarter points if desired.

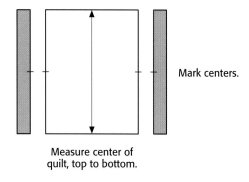

Mark centers.

Measure center of
quilt, top to bottom.

2. Pin the borders to the sides of the quilt top, matching the pins and the ends. Sew the borders in place, easing as necessary. Press the seams toward the border.

3. Measure the width of the quilt top through the center, including the side borders just added. Cut border strips to that measurement. Mark, pin, and sew the borders in place as described above. Press the seams toward the border.

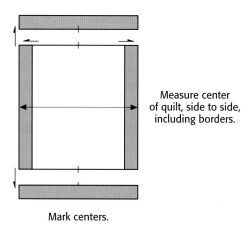

Measure center
of quilt, side to side,
including borders.

Mark centers.

Borders with Corner Squares

In this type of border, you will use shorter border strips because you're adding a corner square. Corner squares also give you the opportunity to use another color in the border.

1. Measure the width and length of the quilt top through the center. Cut border strips to those measurements. Mark the centers of the quilt-top edges and the centers of the border strips (you can also mark quarter points).

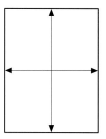

2. Pin the side borders to opposite sides of the quilt, matching the pins and ends and easing as necessary. Stitch in place and press the seams toward the borders. Sew a corner square to each end of the remaining border strips. Press the seams toward the border strip. Pin the borders to the top and bottom edges, matching the centers, seams, and ends. Ease as necessary. Stitch in place and press the seams toward the border.

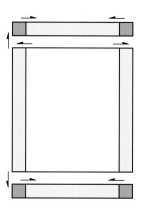

Backing

Choosing backing fabrics can be fun. You can repeat a fabric you've used on the front of the quilt, or you can choose a different fabric that coordinates with the front. Backings don't have to be flannel. If you want a lightweight quilt, perhaps a "summer cover," choose a nonflannel fabric for the back. Homespun-looking fabrics coordinate well with the cozy look and feel of flannels, and these are the fabrics I usually choose if I want a nonflannel backing.

Cut the backing 4" to 6" longer and wider than the quilt top. This allows for any shifting of the layers that may occur during quilting and for the slight shrinkage that occurs when the layers are quilted. Most quilt backings in this book need to be pieced. Unless otherwise noted, a vertical seam will work. Where necessary, I have indicated a horizontal seam. Horizontal seams may require less backing fabric than vertical seams.

If the backing needs to be only a few inches wider than the quilt top, I often add a strip down the middle. The strip can be a single piece of fabric, or it can be pieced from leftover blocks, squares, and rectangles.

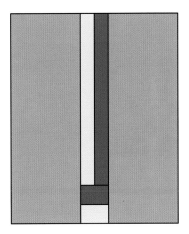

Piecing the Backing from Leftovers

Instead of buying fabric, consider piecing the backing, using larger pieces of fabric left over from the front of the quilt. To do this, cut leftover fabrics into strips or squares. Sew them together randomly or in an interesting pattern until you achieve the required size. If you have leftover blocks from the front, these can be pieced into the back as well.

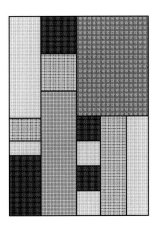

Batting

You have many batting choices. Polyester and cotton battings are the most widely used. I prefer cotton battings for my quilts, including my flannel ones. Cotton battings are flat, easy to quilt, and a heavier weight than polyester, helping wall quilts, in particular, to hang well. Cotton battings are also denser than polyester battings, so I choose a thin one if I want to hand quilt. If you prefer puffier battings, choose a medium- or low-loft polyester.

Cotton battings now come in a range of thicknesses, just like polyester. My favorite is Quilter's Dream Cotton for the thinner battings. "Request:" is the thinnest; "Select" is just a little thicker. For thicker cotton battings, my favorite is Warm & Natural. I do not preshrink my cotton battings. I like the look achieved by the slight shrinkage of a cotton batting when I wash my quilt for the first time. It then looks like my grandmother's quilts. Like the backing, the batting needs to be cut 4" to 6" larger than the quilt top.

Making the Quilt Sandwich

The quilt sandwich is made up of the quilt top, the batting, and the backing. Place the backing, wrong side up, on a large table. Use masking tape to anchor it to the table. Make sure the backing is flat and wrinkle-free, but be careful not to stretch it out of shape. Place the batting on top of the backing, smoothing it well. Center the pressed quilt top, right side up, on top of the batting. Smooth out any wrinkles. Baste with safety pins if you are machine quilting, or thread if you are hand quilting. If you are using pins, do not place them in the areas you intend to quilt.

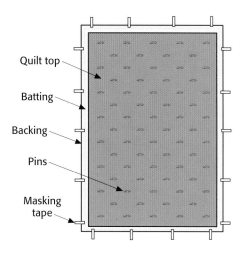

Quilt top
Batting
Backing
Pins
Masking tape

If you are taking your quilt to a professional machine quilter (an increasingly popular option), you will not need to make the quilt sandwich. You will take your quilt top and quilt backing (seamed if necessary) to the quilter. You may be able to purchase the batting directly from her at less than the retail cost because she will only charge you for what your quilt needs. When you buy a packaged batting in a quilt shop, you often have to buy a larger piece than you need, resulting in a leftover piece.

Quilting

Whether you quilt your quilts or someone else does it for you, there are many ways to quilt and many designs from which to choose. Deciding on one out of all your options is often more difficult than doing the quilting. You can machine quilt, hand quilt, or have someone else machine or hand quilt. You can use regular quilting thread, match thread to your fabrics, use decorative threads, or even use pearl cotton.

Machine Quilting

Quilting straight lines is perhaps the easiest way to quilt, especially if you are doing it yourself and are new to machine quilting.

You'll need a walking foot to help feed the quilt layers through the machine without causing them to shift or pucker. The Pfaff sewing machine has a built-in walking foot, called a dual feed, that I love. Other machines require a separate attachment.

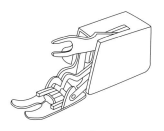

Walking foot

Use straight-line quilting to stitch straight lines, to outline a shape, or to quilt in-the-ditch (in the seam).

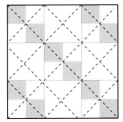

Diagonal straight lines

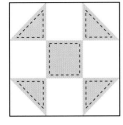

Outline quilt

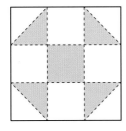

Quilt in the ditch

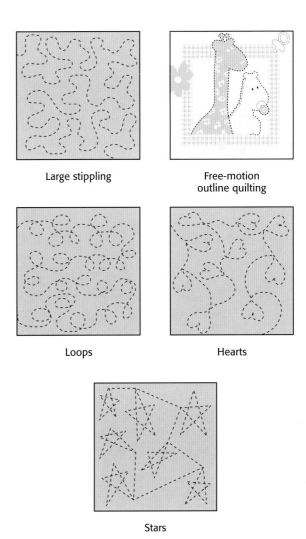

Large stippling

Free-motion outline quilting

Loops

Hearts

Stars

No. 8 pearl cotton can be used for machine quilting. Use a Schmetz Topstitch needle (130N), size 100/16. For No. 12 pearl cotton, use an 80/12 needle.

For free-motion quilting, the most common method is stippling. You will need a darning foot and the ability to drop the feed dogs on your sewing machine. With free-motion quilting, you guide the fabric in the direction you want it to go. This technique requires some practice. Make sure you take the time to machine quilt some samples before you start quilting on your quilt.

Free-motion quilting can be used to stipple, outline a motif in the fabric, or create loops, hearts, and many other designs. See Maurine Noble's book *Machine Quilting Made Easy* (That Patchwork Place, 1994) for more information on machine quilting.

Hand Quilting

Hand quilting takes longer to do than machine quilting, but if you like handwork, you may prefer to hand quilt. Generally, quilters thread-baste quilts for hand quilting. Then they use a hand-quilting thread and a needle called a "between." As with machine quilting, following ¼" away from seam lines or stitching around pieced or appliquéd shapes is an easy guideline.

Pearl cotton can be used for hand quilting if you like the folk-art look. This look coordinates well with flannel quilts. Use a No. 8 pearl cotton and a size 24 chenille needle. You won't be able to load your needle with stitches like you can in traditional hand quilting, and your stitches will be larger than regular quilting stitches, but this type of quilting adds a homey feeling to your quilts.

Binding

I prefer a double-fold, straight-grain binding. I use a double-fold, bias binding only when I want to show off a stripe or a plaid. Bias binding requires more fabric than straight-grain binding. In the quilt directions, I have indicated when bias binding was used. If you don't see the word "bias" in the binding, it is cut on the straight grain.

1. For straight-grain binding strips, cut the required number of 2"-wide strips across the width of the fabric. You will need enough strips to go around the outside edge of the quilt plus extra for the folded corners. Piece the strips together on the diagonal. Press the seams open.

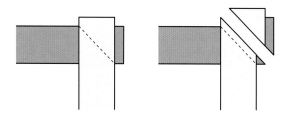

2. Cut one end at a 45° angle. Don't measure, just eyeball it. Fold about ¼" of the angled edge to the wrong side. Press. Iron the entire strip, wrong sides together.

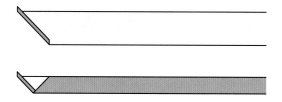

3. Begin on a straight edge of the quilt, away from a corner. Align the raw edges of the binding with the raw edges of the quilt. Begin stitching approximately 3" from the angled end, using a ¼"-wide seam. Backstitch at the beginning for added strength.

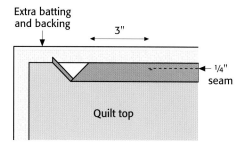

4. When you get close to the corner, insert a pin ¼" from the edge (just eyeball it); sew up to the pin and backstitch. Remove the quilt from the machine.

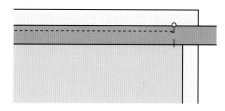

5. Fold the binding up, away from the quilt; then fold the binding back down onto itself. Align the fold along the edge you just stitched. Align the raw edges of the binding with the next edge you'll stitch. Begin stitching at the edge of the quilt top, not ¼" in.

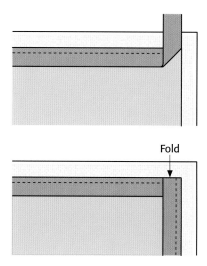

6. Work around all 4 corners of the quilt, just as you did above. When you get close to where you started, insert the binding strip inside the angled end, trimming if it's too long. Continue stitching a little past where you began.

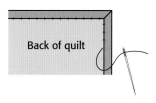

7. Fold the binding to the back. Finish the back by hand with a slip stitch, using thread to match the binding. In the corners, there will be a natural miter on the front. On the back, you will fold the binding into a miter.

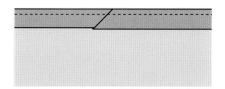

Adding a Label

It is important to label your quilts. This can be done simply and quickly. Use a fine-point permanent marker (size .03 or .05) to write directly on the back of your quilt if the fabric is light in color. I stitch the binding first; then I use it as a straight edge and write along it. If you need or want to make a separate label, choose a simple shape, like a heart, and write (or stitch if you prefer) your name, city, state, and the date (usually just the year) you finished your quilt. Stitch your label to the back of the finished quilt.

The most important thing about a label is to just do it. In future years, you'll be glad you did. How many of us have a family quilt with none of the above information? A label that tells who made the quilt, where, and when adds to the quilt's value, both monetarily and sentimentally.

Embellishing with Buttons

It isn't necessary to add buttons (or other embellishments) to most quilts, but they add dimension, create interest, and makes great animal eyes. For examples of how buttons can be used, see "100 Squares" (page 26) and "Playful Puppies" (page 44). Before adding any buttons, consider how the quilt will be used. Buttons should never be used on quilts for babies or small children. Substitute stitching, such as French knots, instead. Buttons may look great on a quilt meant for an older child's bed, but you'll probably be repairing them often.

Try turning the buttons over to the wrong side. You may like the back of the button better than the front. The back is often flatter and shows just the outline of the button, whereas the front may include raised edges.

I add buttons after quilting because the thread used to attach them goes through all three quilt layers, making them more secure and easier to repair. However, when you add them after quilting, knots are harder to hide. You can put knots on the back and cover them with buttons, put them on the top and leave the tails, or hide the knots between the buttons and the quilt top.

Bibliography

Bonsib, Sandy. *Folk Art Quilts: A Fresh Look.* Bothell, Wash.: Martingale & Company, 1998.

Brackman, Barbara. *Clues in the Calico.* McLean, Va.: EPM Publications, Inc., 1989.

Hargrave, Harriet. *From Fiber to Fabric.* Lafayette, Calif.: C&T Publishing, 1997.

Noble, Maurine. *Machine Quilting Made Easy.* Bothell, Wash.: That Patchwork Place, 1994.

Reikes, Ursula. *Quilts for Baby: Easy as ABC.* Bothell, Wash.: That Patchwork Place, 1993.

_____. *More Quilts for Baby: Easy as ABC.* Bothell, Wash.: That Patchwork Place, 1997.

_____. *Even More Quilts for Baby: Easy as ABC.* Bothell, Wash.: Martingale & Company, 2000.

Shaeffer, Claire B. *Fabric Sewing Guide.* Radnor, Pa.: Chilton Book Co., 1989.

Waldvogel, Merikay. "A Flag Quilt Launches a Search into the Past." *Quilting Today Magazine,* Issue 68, August 12, 1998.

About the Author

Sandy Bonsib is a teacher by profession and a quilter by passion. She has a graduate degree in education and has taught locally at In The Beginning Fabrics in Seattle since 1993 and nationally since 1997. She is the author of three books: *Folk Art Quilts: A Fresh Look* (Martingale & Company, 1998), *Quilting Your Memories: Inspirations for Designing with Image Transfers* (Martingale & Company, 1999), and *Quilting More Memories: Creating Projects with Image Transfers* (Martingale & Company, 2000). This is her fourth book. She has also had quilts published in numerous magazines, most frequently in *American Patchwork & Quilting*. She has appeared on *Lap Quilting with Georgia Bonesteel* (1999) and *Simply Quilts with Alex Anderson* (2000 and 2001), and was one of six featured artists on "Quilts of the Northwest, 1998."

Through In The Beginning Fabrics, Sandy coordinates Quilts for the Children, a group that makes quilts for the children of battered women. For the past three years, she has also been a mentor for high school seniors working on their senior projects in quiltmaking.

Sandy lives on a small farm on Cougar Mountain in Issaquah, Washington, with her husband, John; two teenagers, Ben and Kate; and many animals. She also raises puppies for Guide Dogs for the Blind.

For information about Sandy's classes and lectures, fax her at 425-644-1392 or e-mail her at sjbonsib@aol.com.

NEW AND BESTSELLING TITLES FROM

America's Best-Loved Craft & Hobby Books™

America's Best-Loved Quilt Books®

QUILTING
From That Patchwork Place, an imprint of Martingale & Company

Appliqué
Artful Appliqué
Colonial Appliqué
Red and Green: An Appliqué Tradition
Rose Sampler Supreme
Your Family Heritage: Projects in Appliqué

Baby Quilts
Appliqué for Baby
The Quilted Nursery
Quilts for Baby: Easy as ABC
More Quilts for Baby: Easy as ABC
Even More Quilts for Baby: Easy as ABC

Holiday Quilts
Easy and Fun Christmas Quilts
Favorite Christmas Quilts from That Patchwork Place
Paper Piece a Merry Christmas
A Snowman's Family Album Quilt
Welcome to the North Pole

Learning to Quilt
Basic Quiltmaking Techniques for:
  Borders and Bindings
  Curved Piecing
  Divided Circles
  Eight-Pointed Stars
  Hand Appliqué
  Machine Appliqué
  Strip Piecing
The Joy of Quilting
The Quilter's Handbook
Your First Quilt Book (or it should be!)

Paper Piecing
50 Fabulous Paper-Pieced Stars
A Quilter's Ark
Easy Machine Paper Piecing
Needles and Notions
Paper-Pieced Curves
Show Me How to Paper Piece

Rotary Cutting
101 Fabulous Rotary-Cut Quilts
365 Quilt Blocks a Year Perpetual Calendar
Fat Quarter Quilts
Lap Quilting Lives!
Quick Watercolor Quilts
Quilts from Aunt Amy
Spectacular Scraps
Time-Crunch Quilts

Small & Miniature Quilts
Bunnies By The Bay Meets Little Quilts
Celebrate! with Little Quilts
Easy Paper-Pieced Miniatures
Little Quilts All Through the House

CRAFTS
From Martingale & Company

300 Papermaking Recipes
The Art of Handmade Paper and Collage
The Art of Stenciling
Creepy Crafty Halloween
Gorgeous Paper Gifts
Grow Your Own Paper
Stamp with Style
Wedding Ribbonry

KNITTING
From Martingale & Company

Comforts of Home
Fair Isle Sweaters Simplified
Knit It Your Way
Simply Beautiful Sweaters
Two Sticks and a String
The Ultimate Knitter's Guide
Welcome Home: Kaffe Fassett

COLLECTOR'S COMPASS™
From Martingale & Company

20th Century Glass
'50s Decor
Barbie® Doll
Jewelry
20th Century Dinnerware
United States Coins
Movie Collectibles
'60s and '70s Decor

Our books are available at bookstores and your favorite craft, fabric, yarn, and antiques retailers. If you don't see the title you're looking for, visit us at **www.martingale-pub.com** or contact us at:

1-800-426-3126
International: 1-425-483-3313
Fax: 1-425-486-7596
E-mail: info@martingale-pub.com

For more information and a full list of our titles, visit our Web site or call for a free catalog.